SRA
Open Court Reading
Skills Practice

Grade 2

McGraw Hill Education

Send all inquiries to:
McGraw-Hill Education
8787 Orion Place
Columbus, OH 43240

ISBN: 978-0-07-669304-7
MHID: 0-07-669304-X

Printed in the United States of America

1 2 3 4 5 6 7 8 9 QVS 20 19 18 17 16 15

Table of Contents

Unit 6 Storytelling

/ō/ spelled _ow, oa_, o, and o_e

> **FOCUS** The /ō/ sound can be spelled _ow, oa_, o, and o_e.

PRACTICE Use the equations to add (+) and remove (–) letters to create different /ō/ words.

1. glow – g + f = _____ – f + b = _____

2. poke – p + j = _____ – j + sp = _____

3. grow – g + c = _____ – c + th = _____

4. road – r + t = _____ – t + l = _____

5. host – h + p = _____ – p + m = _____

6. coat – c + b = _____ – b + m = _____

Write two sentences using words from the equations above. Circle the /ō/ spelling pattern in each word you choose.

7. _____

_____

8. _____

_____

APPLY Choose a word from the box to complete each sentence.

hollow	oak	bone	throat	mow
oval	vote	frozen	yellow	loaf

9. We can ice-skate on the _____ pond.

10. Rabbits made a nest in the _____ log.

11. Anna gets paid to _____ the grass.

12. Luke has a fever and a sore _____.

13. We _____ for class president next week.

14. The warm _____ of bread smells wonderful.

15. Let's rest under the giant _____ tree.

16. Barkley hid his _____ in the backyard.

17. The racetrack has an _____ shape.

18. The large, _____ bus stopped to pick us up.

Compound Words, Synonyms, and Antonyms

FOCUS
- A **compound word** is made when two words are put together to make a new word. For example: gold + fish = goldfish
- **Synonyms** are words that are similar in meaning. *Tired* and *sleepy* are synonyms.
- **Antonyms** are words that are opposite in meaning. *Bad* and *good* are antonyms.

PRACTICE Combine the words below to make a *compound word*. Write the new word on the line.

1. table + cloth = _____

2. home + work = _____

3. lady + bug = _____

Draw a line to match each word to its *synonym*.

4. choose   **a.** giggle

5. ill   **b.** select

6. laugh   **c.** sick

Draw a line to match each word to its *antonym*.

7. before   **a.** work

8. over   **b.** after

9. play   **c.** under

APPLY Fill in each blank with a *compound word*.

10. A bath for a bird is a _____.

11. A pot to put tea in is a _____.

12. Light that comes from the sun is _____.

13. A cone that comes from a pine tree is a _____.

14. A cake that is made in a cup is a _____.

Write a *synonym* for the word in parentheses ( ) to complete the sentence.

15. (angry) Mr. Banks was _____ that we broke the window.

16. (seat) Sit on the _____ next to Tori.

17. (shout) I had to _____ so Dad could hear me over the lawnmower.

Write an *antonym* for the word in parentheses ( ) to complete the sentence.

18. (gloomy) Lots of people go to the park on a _____ day.

19. (last) We were _____ in line to get tickets for the show.

20. (close) The weather is warm enough for me to _____ my window.

Vocabulary

> **FOCUS** Review the vocabulary words from "Flower Power."

advance   exhale   oxygen
carbon dioxide   minerals   pollen
comfortable   nutritious   produce
develop   observe   transfer

PRACTICE Write the vocabulary word that matches each clue.

1. Plants take this in from the air. _____

2. People take this in from the air. _____

3. A healthful meal is this. _____

4. Plants get these small pieces from good soil.
   _____

5. When you breathe out, you do this. _____

6. If you use tongs to pick up a piece of food and move it to
   a new dish, you do this. _____

7. If you sink into a big, soft chair, you are probably
   this. _____

8. If you carefully watch the movement of ants, you do
   this. _____

APPLY A *base word* is a word that can stand alone. Endings are added to base words to change their meanings.

Write each word that has a vocabulary word for its base. Then write the vocabulary word that is the base word.

9. Insects help to pollinate flowers.

Which word contains the vocabulary word? _____

What is its base word? _____

10. A growth chart measures development.

Which word contains the vocabulary word? _____

What is its base word? _____

11. The advancement of the mudslide put the houses in danger.

Which word contains the vocabulary word? _____

What is its base word? _____

12. The production studio made a new movie.

Which word contains the vocabulary word? _____

What is its base word? _____

Cause and Effect

FOCUS • A *cause* is why something happens.
• An *effect* is what happens.

PRACTICE **Read each sentence. Write the *effect*
(what happened) and the *cause* (why it happened).**

1. Because the woman planted seeds, flowers grew in
her garden.

Effect: _____

Cause: _____

2. Because the bees gathered nectar from the flowers, they
were able to make honey.

Effect: _____

Cause: _____

3. Because the bees made honey, they had food during
the winter.

Effect: _____

Cause: _____

4. Because the bees made honey, the beekeeper was able to
gather some.

Effect: _____

Cause: _____

APPLY Look at "Flower Power" for the *effects* listed below. Then write the *cause* for each one.

5. **Effect:** The nutritious soil makes the plant stronger.

   Cause: _____

6. **Effect:** There is oxygen for people to breathe.

   Cause: _____

7. **Effect:** There is carbon dioxide for plants to take in.

   Cause: _____

8. **Look at Chapter 2 of "Flower Power." Write one *cause* and its *effect* from this chapter.**

   Cause: _____

   Effect: _____

Writing to Inform

Think

Audience: *Who* will read your writing?

_____

Purpose: *What* is your reason for writing?

_____

Prewriting

Use the Venn diagram below to plan your comparing and contrasting text. Write comparisons in the overlapping section of the diagram. Then write contrasts in the outer sections.

Topic:_____   Topic:_____

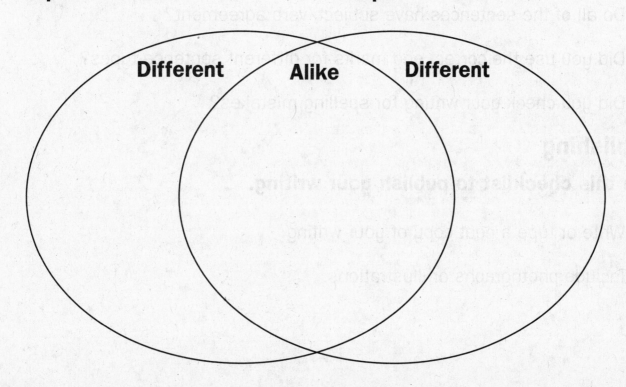

Revising

Use this checklist to revise your writing.

- [ ] Did you include compare and contrast signal words?

- [ ] Did you include linking words to organize your facts and explanations?

- [ ] Did you include descriptive words and details?

- [ ] Did you vary the lengths of your sentences?

- [ ] Did you include a concluding sentence?

- [ ] Does your writing have a clear purpose?

Editing/Proofreading

Use this checklist to correct mistakes in your writing.

- [ ] Did you use proofreading symbols when editing?

- [ ] Did you indent each new paragraph?

- [ ] Do all of the sentences have subject/verb agreement?

- [ ] Did you use the correct end marks for different sentence types?

- [ ] Did you check your writing for spelling mistakes?

Publishing

Use this checklist to publish your writing.

- [ ] Write or type a neat copy of your writing.

- [ ] Include photographs or illustrations.

APPLY **Replace the underlined letter or letters to create a spelling word with the same /ō/ sound. Write the word on the line.**

13. <u>sh</u>one + st = _____

14. <u>r</u>ow + sh = _____

15. <u>m</u>ow + bl = _____

16. goat + b = _____

17. th<u>r</u>ow + kn = _____

Write the correct spelling word on the line. Use the words in the box.

notebook	hello	flown	oatmeal	stroke

18. Please say _____ to your mother when you see her.

19. I love to have warm _____ for breakfast on a cold day.

20. Zack wrote the math problems in his _____.

21. It was time to leave at the _____ of midnight.

22. I have never _____ on an airplane before.

/ō/ spelled _ow, oa_, o, and o_e; Synonyms and Antonyms; Compound Words

FOCUS
- The /ō/ sound can be spelled _ow, oa_, o, and o_e.
- Compound words are made up of two smaller words.

  Example: cow + boy = cowboy

PRACTICE Sort the spelling words. Some words will be used more than once.

/ō/ spelled _ow

1. _____
2. _____
3. _____
4. _____

/ō/ spelled oa_

5. _____
6. _____

/ō/ spelled o

7. _____

/ō/ spelled o_

8. _____
9. _____
10. _____

Compound word

11. _____
12. _____

Word List		Challenge Words
1. stone	6. know	11. borrow
2. flown	7. blow	12. coast
3. notebook	8. hello	13. goldfish
4. stroke	9. oatmeal	14. owe
5. boat	10. show	15. loan

Adverbs

FOCUS
- **Adverbs** are words that describe verbs by telling *how*, *where*, or *when*.

  Examples:
  We must run **quickly.** (how)
  I like to run **outside.** (where)
  I **always** run with my friends. (when)

PRACTICE Read the sentence. Circle the *adverbs*.

1. The corner store is always open.

2. Shoppers quickly find the items they need.

3. Cashiers eagerly wait for customers.

4. The butcher happily serves people the meat they want.

5. My mother waits outside while I go inside to buy fruit.

Write an *adverb* to describe each *verb*.

6. play (where) _____

7. talk (when) _____

8. move (how) _____

APPLY Read the paragraph below. Circle the *adverbs*.

Markets have always been a part of communities. Markets provide quality food, goods, and services to people. They are convenient and can quickly provide customers with milk, eggs, or bread. The owners of markets have a desire to provide friendly service. Customers can easily find items they want at the market because the aisles are marked. Soon flowers will be able to be found outside the market. My favorite section of the market is the brightly colored fruits and vegetables. Tomorrow I will go to the market.

In the sentences below, circle the correct word and then identify it as an *adjective* or *adverb*.

9. The (jealous, jealously) girl wanted to go on vacation with her friend. _____

10. He (obedient, obediently) listened to his mother. _____

11. Amelia entered the forest very (brave, bravely). _____

In the sentences below, identify the *part of speech* of the underlined word. Then tell which word it *modifies*.

12. I <u>often</u> go to my neighbor's house. _____ _____

13. Jessica is <u>very</u> sad. _____ _____

14. My dog <u>always</u> finishes his dinner. _____ _____

/ū/ spelled _ew, _ue, u, and u_e

FOCUS The /ū/ sound can be spelled _ew, _ue, u, and u_e.

PRACTICE Read the following words aloud.

cue	pew	humor	compute
unit	amuse	value	curfew

Write the words with /ū/ spelled like _hue._

1. _____ 2. _____

Write the words with /ū/ spelled like _few._

3. _____ 4. _____

Write the words with /ū/ spelled like _music._

5. _____ 6. _____

Write the words with /ū/ spelled like _cute._

7. _____ 8. _____

APPLY Circle the word with /ū/ in each
sentence. Write the word and its /ū/ spelling
pattern on the lines.

9. Lexi is always home before her curfew.

_____   _____

10. Did Max use all of the cups?

_____   _____

11. A police officer came to the rescue!

_____   _____

12. Was the stolen art returned to the museum?

_____   _____

13. A sunny day is good for a barbecue.

_____   _____

14. Water spewed from the broken hose.

_____   _____

15. Gus gave his dog a huge hug.

_____   _____

16. Angela refuses to give up.

_____   _____

Multiple-Meaning Words

> **FOCUS** **Multiple-meaning words** are spelled and
> pronounced the same but have different
> meanings. **Example:**
> **bark** Meaning 1: the sound a dog makes
> Meaning 2: the outer coating on a tree

PRACTICE Use the multiple-meaning words below
to complete the sentences. Use each word twice.

kind	last	sink

1. Hugo is always _____. What _____ of pizza do
   you like?

2. A hole in the boat will cause it to _____. The dishes
   in the _____ still need to be washed.

3. December is the _____ month of the year. These
   sneakers will not _____ another year.

APPLY Read the two meanings for a multiple-meaning
word. Write the word on the line.

4. a deep, round dish for holding liquids **or** to play a game by
   knocking down pins with a ball _____

5. to cram or wedge into something **or** a type of jelly _____

6. a water bird with a bill and webbed feet that quacks **or** to lower
   or bend down quickly _____

Homophones

FOCUS **Homophones** are words that are pronounced the same but have different spellings and meanings.
Example: I <u>see</u> a dolphin swimming in the <u>sea</u>.

PRACTICE Use these *homophones* to complete the sentences.

we'll	rowed	cents
wheel	road	sense

7. A gumball costs 50 _____. Use your _____ of smell to sniff the perfume.

8. The wagon won't roll if it's missing a _____. If we study tonight, _____ be ready for the test tomorrow.

9. A car stopped at the side of the _____. Henry and Rachel _____ their boat to shore.

APPLY Read the two meanings for a pair of homophones. Write the *homophones* on the lines.

10. the number after seven _____

    past tense of *eat* _____

11. the opposite of *yes* _____

    to understand _____

12. using the voice to be heard _____

    to be permitted _____

Vocabulary

FOCUS Review the vocabulary words from "Hungry Little Hare."

blend	only	snoopy
drowsy	prying	stump
exactly	scent	tender
hind	slender	wily

PRACTICE *Synonyms* are words that mean the same or nearly the same thing. Match each vocabulary word with its synonym below.

1. drowsy   **a.** sleepy

2. prying   **b.** tricky

3. scent   **c.** snoopy

4. tender   **d.** soft

5. slender   **e.** smell

6. wily   **f.** thin

APPLY Circle the vocabulary word that completes each sentence in the passage below.

The chipmunk has stripes that help it **7.** (blend, prying) into the shadows. The Native American Iroquois tribe told a story explaining the chipmunk's stripes. In this story, Bear is very proud of his strength. **8.** (Drowsy, Snoopy) Chipmunk overhears Bear.

He asks Bear if his strength can stop the sun from rising. Bear decides to try, and commands the sun not to rise. However, the sun rises **9.** (drowsy, exactly) as it always has.

Bear is so angry that he traps Chipmunk under his huge **10.** (slender, hind) paw. **11.** (Prying, Wily) Chipmunk has an idea to trick Bear. He asks Bear to only lift the paw up a little, just so he can speak.

Then Chipmunk slides out of the **12.** (snoopy, slender) space and runs away. As he runs, a **13.** (scent, stump) trips him and slows him down.

Instead of catching Chipmunk again, Bear **14.** (only, exactly) swipes Chipmunk with three claws. This leaves three stripes forever on Chipmunk's back.

Sequence

FOCUS
- *Sequence* is the order in which events in a story occur.
  Writers often use time-and-order words to help readers understand the sequence of events.
- *Time* words (*winter, moment, morning*) show the passage of time.
- *Order* words (*first, next, finally*) show the order in which events happen.

PRACTICE **Read this paragraph carefully. Write the *time* and *order* words on the lines below.**

The moment the little rabbit awoke that morning, she first stretched and yawned. Next, she sniffed the air. Something smelled different. She hopped out of her burrow and looked at the wide world. What had changed? Then she realized—the snow was beginning to melt. Winter was finally turning into spring.

Time words

1. _____

2. _____

3. _____

4. _____

Order words

5. _____

6. _____

7. _____

8. _____

**_APPLY_ Think about the plot of "Hungry Little Hare."
Use what you know from the text to answer the
sequence questions below.**

9. What happened first that caused Little Hare to begin
to hop? _____

**Recount, or tell, the order in which Little Hare sees
the hidden animals. Use the order words _first, next,_
and _finally_.**

10. _____

11. _____

12. _____

13. _____

14. _____

15. _____

**Most of the story happens during late summer. Then
there is a final illustration in which Little Hare looks
very different and it is winter. Make an educated
guess to infer what happened to Little Hare during
the fall.**

16. _____

Access Complex Text • _Skills Practice 2_

Writing to Inform

Think

Audience: *Who* will read your research report?

_____

Purpose: *What* is your reason for writing a research report?

_____

Prewriting

Use the graphic organizer below to brainstorm questions you could answer about your topic.

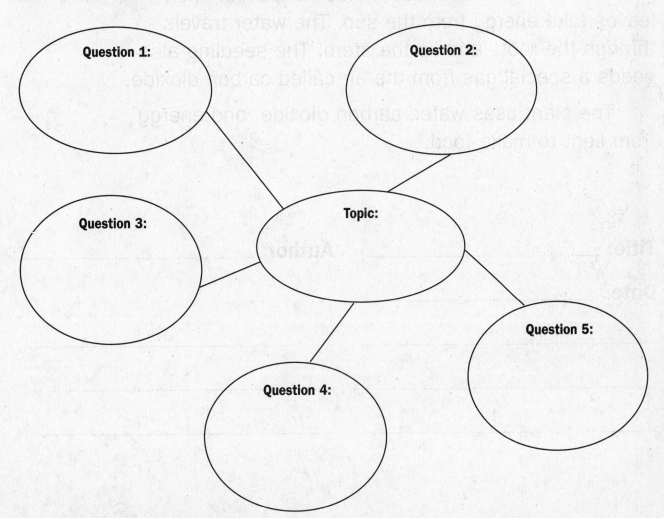

Taking Notes

PRACTICE Use the lines below to take notes from the following paragraphs of "Flower Power" by Julia Wall.

"Worms and other animals help make the soil more nutritious. This makes the plant stronger. A healthier plant is better food for animals and people.

A stem and leaves also come out of the seed. They advance through the soil toward the light. The plant will need energy from sunlight.

The young plant bursts out of the soil. It grows taller and taller and becomes a seedling.

A seedling makes food inside its leaves. The leaves take energy from the sun. The water travels through the roots and up the stem. The seedling also needs a special gas from the air called carbon dioxide.

The plant uses water, carbon dioxide, and energy from light to make food."

Title: _____   Author: _____

Date: _____

_____   _____

_____   _____

_____   _____

/ū/ spelled _ew, _ue, u, u_e; Homophones and Multiple-Meaning Words

> ## FOCUS
> • Some ways /ū/ can be spelled are _ew, _ue, u, and u_e.
> • Homophones are words that sound the same but have different spellings and meanings.
> **Example:** I took a *peek* at the answers. We climbed to the *peak* of the mountain.

PRACTICE Sort the spelling words.

/ū/ spelled _ew

1. _____

2. _____

/ū/ spelled _ue

3. _____

4. _____

/ū/ spelled u

5. _____

/ū/ spelled u_e

6. _____

Homophones

7. _____

8. _____

9. _____

10. _____

Word List		Challenge Words
1. hair	**6.** cell	**11.** uniform
2. hue	**7.** sell	**12.** confuse
3. few	**8.** cute	**13.** view
4. hare	**9.** human	**14.** pupils
5. pew	**10.** rescue	**15.** statue

APPLY Circle the correct spelling for each spelling
word. Write the correct spelling on the line.

11. pue   pew   _____

12. cute   kute   _____

13. reskew   rescue   _____

14. fue   few   _____

15. hew   hue   _____

**Circle the misspelled word in each sentence. Write the
word correctly on the line.**

16. Every yoomun has a special value. _____

17. We will cell fruit baskets as a fundraiser for our soccer
team. _____

18. There was a hair hopping along in the garden.
_____

19. I got my hare cut. _____

20. A red blood sell carries oxygen. _____

Collective Nouns

> **FOCUS**
> - A **collective noun** describes a group of specific people, animals, or things.
> - Even though they describe groups that are made up of more than one person, animal, or thing, collective nouns are singular nouns. Collective nouns need singular verbs for a sentence to have subject/verb agreement.

PRACTICE Read each sentence. Write *C* for *Correct* if the verb agrees in number with the subject. Write *I* for *Incorrect* if the verb does NOT agree in number with the subject.

1. A troop of monkeys are following the bus through the village. _____

2. The flock of sparrows lands on the ground. _____

3. The brood of hens returns to the coop. _____

4. A large school of fish are swimming in the aquarium. _____

5. The bouquet of flowers have a lovely smell. _____

6. A colony of bats swarms out of the cave at dusk. _____

APPLY Choose a *collective noun* from the box to complete each sentence.

team	panel	herd	litter	pack

7. A _____ of cattle is heading to pasture.

8. The _____ of puppies is adorable.

9. We could hear the _____ of wolves howling most of the night.

10. A _____ of judges is choosing the best painting of the art show.

11. The _____ of oxen drags the plow across the field.

Write a sentence using each collective noun as the subject. Be sure each verb agrees in number with the subject.

12. pride of lions

_____

13. family of bears

_____

14. crowd of people

_____

15. group of students

_____

/ō/ spelled _ow, oa_, o and o_e

> **FOCUS** The /ō/ sound can be spelled _ow, oa_, o, and o_e.

PRACTICE Read the following words aloud.
Underline the /ō/ spelling or spellings in each word.

1. rodeo   4. explode

2. overflow   5. roadblock

3. ozone   6. boatload

APPLY Write one of the words from above to complete each sentence.

7. Don't let the bath water _____ from the tub!

8. Cars were forced to turn around at the _____.

9. Barrel racing is an event at the _____.

10. The _____ layer helps protect life on Earth.

11. That volcano will _____ soon.

12. We bought a _____ of clothes during the sale.

/ū/ spelled _ew, _ue, u, and u_e

> **FOCUS** The /ū/ sound can be spelled _ew, _ue, u, and u_e.

PRACTICE Read the following word pairs.
Circle the word with /ū/.

13. full   fuel

14. abuse   abrupt

15. continent   continue

16. humid   hummed

17. volume   volunteer

18. cupped   cupid

APPLY Draw a line to connect the rhyming words.

19. skews   **a.** venue

20. few   **b.** contribute

21. menu   **c.** pew

22. distribute   **d.** fuse

Name _____ **Date** _____

Prefix *dis-*

> **FOCUS**
> - A **prefix** is added to the beginning of a word and changes the meaning of that word.
> - The prefix *dis-* means "the opposite of" or "not."
>   **Example:** dis + comfort = discomfort (the lack or opposite of comfort)

PRACTICE Add the prefix *dis-* to the base words below. Write the new word on the first line. Then write the meaning of the new word.

Base Word	New Word	New Meaning
1. advantage	_____	_____
2. appear	_____	_____
3. order	_____	_____
4. respect	_____	_____

APPLY Write two sentences using the new words from above.

5. _____

_____

6. _____

_____

Prefix *un-*

> **FOCUS**
> - A **prefix** is added to the beginning of a word and changes the meaning of that word.
> - The prefix *un-* means "the opposite of" or "not."
>   **Example:** un + happy = unhappy (not happy)

PRACTICE Add the prefix *un-* to the base words below. Write the new word on the first line. Then write the meaning of the new word.

Base Word	New Word	New Meaning
7. buckle	_____	_____
8. ripe	_____	_____
9. common	_____	_____
10. stuck	_____	_____
11. real	_____	_____

APPLY Fill in the blank with the prefix *dis-* or *un-* to create a new word that makes sense in the sentence.

12. Joe used a key to _____lock the safe.

13. We were _____interested in the boring speech.

14. It is _____safe for the wires to be

_____connected.

Word Analysis • *Skills Practice 2*

Vocabulary

<table>
<tr><td>

FOCUS Review the vocabulary words from "Where's the Honey, Honey?"

</td></tr>
</table>

ancient	**effective**	**wax**
beehive	**flush**	**wilderness**

PRACTICE Read each pair of sentences below. Circle the correct ending to the second sentence.

1. In the game of hide-and-seek, the person seeking others tries to flush them from hiding places. The seeker:

  a. helps others hide. **b.** drives others out.

2. The farmer keeps bees in beehives on her farm. The farmer keeps bees in:

  a. a special kind of bee house. **b.** a special kind of net.

3. National Parks protect areas of wilderness. The parks protect:

  a. city areas with many buildings.

  b. natural areas with few people.

4. The candle maker used wax to make candles. The candle maker used:

  a. a special kind of plastic.

  b. a substance made by honeybees.

APPLY Use a vocabulary word to complete each pair of sentences.

5. Beekeeping is an _____ art. There is evidence that people have kept bees for at least 4,000 years.

6. The first beekeepers decided that, rather than seek hives in the _____, they should find a way to keep bees nearby. This meant people had to build the bees a home.

7. Egyptians of long ago had round, clay hives. They could open the backs of these hives, use smoke to calm and _____ out the bees, and take out honeycombs.

8. The Egyptians then put the combs inside cowhides and trampled them. This separated the honey from the _____.

9. In the Middle Ages in Europe, the skep was a kind of _____ or bee house. People made a skep from straw or rope.

10. People covered it with mud as an _____ way to keep out water. They put it in a small shelf, called a bole, on the side of a wall.

Main Idea and Details

FOCUS • The *main idea* tells what a paragraph is about. It is the most important idea presented by the author.

• *Details* provide more specific information about the *main idea*.

PRACTICE **Read the paragraph. It is missing a main idea sentence.**

Honey can be used to sweeten food. It has a natural ability to kill bacteria, so some people use it as medicine. It can soften people's skin and get rid of dead skin cells. Eating a little honey before a workout can raise athletes' energy levels.

Circle the *best* main idea sentence.

1. a. Honey is delicious. **b.** Honey has many uses.

Write three details from the paragraph that support the main idea.

2. _____

3. _____

4. _____

APPLY Look again at "Where's the Honey, Honey?" Use information from the selection to answer the questions below.

Look at the page with the heading "Both Win." Is this subheading the main idea of this section of text?

5. Circle *yes* or *no*.

Support your answer with two details from the page.

6. _____

_____

7. _____

_____

Look at the last paragraph in the selection.

Write the main idea of this paragraph.

8. _____

_____

Write two details that support this main idea.

9. _____

_____

10. _____

_____

Access Complex Text • *Skills Practice 2*

Vary How Sentences Begin

PRACTICE All of the sentences below begin the same. Rewrite the sentences so the beginnings vary.

1. A tree is a woody plant.

_____

2. A tree uses its roots to get water from the ground.

_____

3. A tree's trunk is protected by bark.

_____

4. A tree produces oxygen.

_____

5. A tree can help prevent erosion.

_____

6. A tree provides shade.

_____

Using Multimedia to Illustrate

Planning

Use the idea web below to brainstorm ideas of how you can use multimedia sources to illustrate your research report.

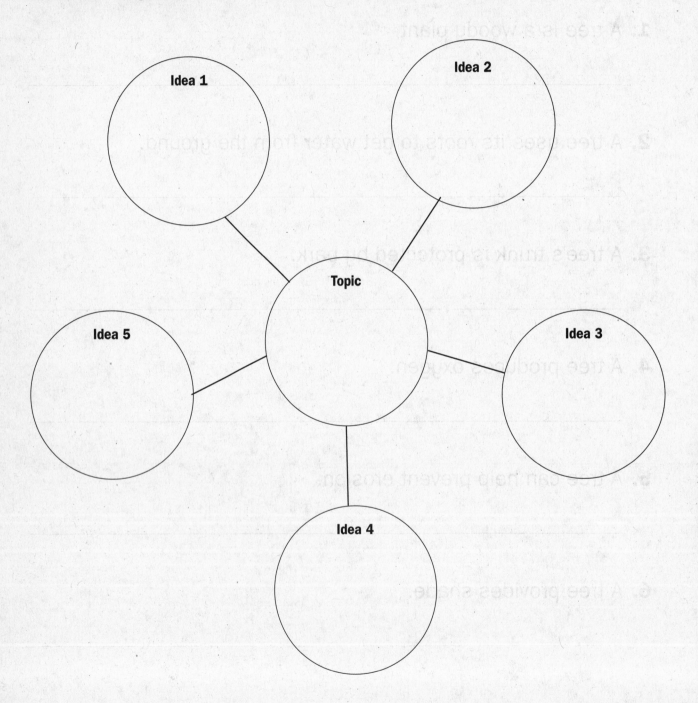

Review /ō/ and /ū/; Prefixes *dis-* and *un-*

FOCUS
- The /ō/ sound can be spelled _ow, oa_, o, and o_e.
- The /ū/ sound can be spelled are _ew, _ue, u, and u_e.
- The prefix *dis-* and *un-* mean "not" or "the opposite of."

PRACTICE Sort the spelling words.

Words with /ō/ sound

1. _____

2. _____

3. _____

Words with /ū/ sound

4. _____

5. _____

6. _____

Words with the prefix *dis-*

7. _____

8. _____

Words with the prefix *un-*

9. _____

10. _____

Word List		**Challenge Words**
1. tow	**6.** fuel	**11.** disobeys
2. humid	**7.** cone	**12.** unzipped
3. disagree	**8.** unlock	**13.** unable
4. soap	**9.** distrust	**14.** cocoa
5. unplanned	**10.** pure	**15.** argue

APPLY Find the spelling word that rhymes with the word or words below.

11. phone   bone   _____

12. so   low   _____

13. rope   scope   _____

14. cruel   mule   _____

15. cure   _____

Complete the sentence below. Choose words from the box.

unlock	unplanned	disagree	humid	distrust

16. I _____ my brother on April Fool's Day because he loves pranks.

17. My friend Caleb was sweating a lot because it was so _____ outside.

18. The pirates could not _____ the treasure chest.

19. Ryan and Jack _____ about who is the greatest basketball player of all time.

20. Uncle Rusty's visit was _____, so my mom ran out to buy more groceries.

Pronouns

FOCUS A **pronoun** is a word that takes the place of a noun (person, place, or thing) in a sentence.

Singular Pronouns: *I, you, he, she, it, me, him, her*
Plural Pronouns: *we, they, them, us*
Reflexive Pronouns: *myself, yourself, himself, herself, yourselves, ourselves, themselves*

Rules:	Examples:
• **Singular nouns** must be replaced with **singular pronouns**.	• **Singular:** The cat sleeps. **It** sleeps.
• **Plural nouns** must be replaced with **plural pronouns**.	• **Plural:** <u>Brianna and Madeline</u> are sisters **They** are sisters.
• **Pronouns** must also match the **gender** of the nouns.	• **Male:** <u>Brian</u> helped cook **He** helped cook.
• **Reflexive pronouns** refer back to the subject of the sentence.	• **Reflexive:** John gave <u>John</u> a haircut. John gave **himself** a haircut.

PRACTICE Write a *pronoun* to replace the underlined noun in each sentence.

1. <u>Jody and I</u> raced our bikes across the park. _____

2. On Saturday, <u>Michael and Anthony</u> went swimming. _____

3. <u>Mom</u> was very surprised with the gifts. _____

4. I gave <u>Brian</u> a poster for the wall. _____

APPLY Circle the *singular pronouns*, and underline the *plural pronouns* in the paragraph.

I thought rabbits and hares were the same because they look alike. You would not believe the differences between them. A hare's fur is special. It turns white in the winter. The fur of rabbits changes from brown to gray with the seasons. A mother rabbit will build a nest for her babies, while hares are born on the ground. If we were to see rabbits in the wild, they would be with a group, but hares live alone. It has been fun for me to learn about these animals.

Write a sentence for each *reflexive pronoun* below. Be sure the subject of the sentence and the pronoun agree in number.

myself	themselves	yourself	himself

5. _____

_____

6. _____

_____

7. _____

_____

8. _____

_____

/o͞o/ spelled oo

FOCUS The /o͞o/ sound can be spelled oo.

PRACTICE Read the sentence. Change the word in the box to make a new rhyming word. Write the new word on the line.

1. | broom | The bride and _____ had a fancy wedding.

2. | moon | We usually eat lunch at _____.

3. | noodle | The little _____ is chasing its tail.

4. | pool | Put on a jacket if the air is too _____.

5. | mood | How much _____ did you pack for the picnic?

6. | boots | A plant's _____ hold it in the dirt.

7. | gloom | Hal's roses _____ in the summer.

8. | goof | Rain leaked in from a hole in the _____.

APPLY Choose a word from the box to complete each sentence. Write the word on the line.

moon	scoop	bedroom	loose	boots
cartoon	zoomed	tools	pool	too

9. Matt prefers to study in his _____.

10. A dentist uses _____ to clean and fix teeth.

11. Let us watch the _____ with a dog named Power Pup.

12. The rocket _____ into the air.

13. A _____ ring might slip off your finger.

14. _____ some food into the cat's dish.

15. Sally needs a warm pair of _____ for the winter.

16. Does Nick's swimming _____ have a diving board?

17. I will go to the party, and Tess will come _____.

18. A full _____ can light up the night.

Prefix *non-*

> **FOCUS**
> - A **prefix** is added to the beginning of a word and changes the meaning of that word.
> - The prefix *non-* means "the opposite of" or "not."
>   **Example:** non + human = nonhuman (not human)

PRACTICE **Add the prefix *non-* to the base words below. Write the new word on the first line. Then write the meaning of the new word.**

Base Word	New Word	New Meaning
1. living	_____	_____
2. fat	_____	_____
3. fiction	_____	_____
4. sense	_____	_____

APPLY **Write two sentences using the new words from above.**

5. _____

_____

6. _____

_____

Prefix re-

FOCUS
- A **prefix** is added to the beginning of a word and changes the meaning of that word.
- The prefix re- means "again" or "back."
  Example: re + play = replay (play again or play back)

PRACTICE Add the prefix re- to the base words below. Write the new word on the first line. Then write the meaning of the new word.

Base Word	New Word	New Meaning
7. call	_____	_____
8. trace	_____	_____
9. turn	_____	_____
10. do	_____	_____
11. write	_____	_____

APPLY Fill in the blank with the prefix non- or re- to create a new word that makes sense in the sentence.

12. Bree wants to _____ join the swim team next summer.

13. Josh uses _____ toxic cleaners that do not harm his skin.

14. We will _____ decorate the room after we _____ paint the walls.

Vocabulary

> **FOCUS** Review the vocabulary words from "Busy Bees."

antenna	invade	products
design	limbs	vacant

PRACTICE Match each word with its definition below.

1. vacant   **a.** feelers

2. invade   **b.** things that are made

3. limbs   **c.** large branches on a tree

4. antenna   **d.** to enter without permission

5. design   **e.** empty

6. products   **f.** to make for a purpose

APPLY Look again at "Busy Bees." Complete each sentence with a vocabulary word, and then answer the question that follows.

7. A bee has an _____ on its head.

What is one thing the bee uses its antenna for?

_____

8. A bee will not let another animal _____ the hive.

If another animal invades, what might it steal from the hive?

_____

9. Bees _____ or make cells inside their hives.

Think about why bees design these cells. What is something bees keep inside them?

_____

10. Some hives hang from the _____ of tall trees.

Why do you think a limb might be a safe place?

_____

Classify and Categorize

> **FOCUS** *Classifying* and *categorizing* help you organize information. It is a way of putting people, animals, and objects into different groups. It can help you see ways things are alike and different. It can also help you remember important ideas.

PRACTICE Think about different types of clothing. Classify them into the following categories. Then explain why they belong in that category.

Warm weather clothing

1. _____ belongs in this category

    because _____

2. _____ belongs in this category

    because _____

Cold weather clothing

3. _____ belongs in this category

    because _____

4. _____ belongs in this category

    because _____

APPLY Look again at "Busy Bees." Think of three categories of bee described in this selection. Then categorize one detail about each bee.

5. One category of bee is _____

6. One detail I could use to categorize this type of bee is

   _____.

7. One category of bee is _____

8. One detail I could use to categorize this type of bee is

   _____.

9. One category of bee is _____

10. One detail I could use to categorize this type of bee is

    _____.

Proofreading Symbols

¶　　Indent the paragraph.

^　　Add something.

℘　　Take out something.

/　　Make a small letter.

≡　　Make a capital letter.

sp　　Check spelling.

⊙　　Add a period.

Revising

Use this checklist to revise your writing.

☐ Did you include a strong opening with an informative topic sentence?

☐ Did you include context clues to help readers understand new words?

☐ Did you use cause-and-effect signal words?

☐ Did you vary the beginnings of sentences?

☐ Did you include interesting and descriptive details?

☐ Did you present the facts and explanations about your topic in a logical sequence?

☐ Did you include a concluding sentence?

Editing/Proofreading

Use this checklist to correct mistakes in your writing.

☐ Did you use proofreading symbols when editing?

☐ Did you indent each new paragraph?

☐ Did you use commas correctly?

☐ Did you use the correct end marks for different sentence types?

☐ Did you check your writing for spelling mistakes?

Publishing

Use this checklist to publish your writing.

☐ Write or type a neat copy of your writing.

☐ Use a multimedia source to add an illustration or other visual element.

/ōō/ spelled *oo*; Prefixes *non-* and *re-*

FOCUS
- The /ōō/ sound sounds like the underlined letters in z<u>oo</u>.
- One way the /ōō/ sound can be spelled is *oo*.
- The prefix *non-* means "not."
- The prefix *re-* means "again" or "back."

PRACTICE Sort the spelling words.

/ōō/ spelled *oo*

1. _____
2. _____
3. _____
4. _____
5. _____
6. _____

Words with the prefix *non-*

7. _____
8. _____

Words with the prefix *re-*

9. _____
10. _____

Word List		**Challenge Words**
1. hoop	**6.** bloom	**11.** nonsense
2. tooth	**7.** food	**12.** school
3. mood	**8.** nonfat	**13.** bedroom
4. nonstop	**9.** repaid	**14.** rooster
5. rewrite	**10.** pool	**15.** recycle

APPLY Replace the underlined letter or letters to create a spelling word.

11. <u>c</u>ool + *p* = _____

12. <u>f</u>ood + *m* = _____

13. <u>b</u>ooth + *t* = _____

14. <u>st</u>oop + *h* = _____

15. <u>r</u>oom + *bl* = _____

Circle the correct spelling for each word below. Then write the correct spelling on the line.

16. repayed   repaid   _____

17. nawnfat   nonfat   _____

18. food   fude   _____

19. rewrite   reerite   _____

20. nawstawp   nonstop   _____

Contractions

> **FOCUS** • A **contraction** combines two words. In a contraction, some letters from one or both of the original words are left out, and an apostrophe (') takes the place of the missing letters.
>
> **Examples:**
> are not—aren't   do not—don't
> I am—I'm   she is—she's
> could have—could've   would have—would've

PRACTICE Circle the correct *contraction* in each sentence below.

1. Greenland **isn't/don't** a continent.

2. There **won't/aren't** a lot of people living in Greenland.

3. Hawaii **wasn't/weren't** a state until 1959.

4. I **won't/haven't** be attending the event.

5. I **wouldn't/haven't** heard any information on the test.

6. Tomorrow there **won't/aren't** be a test.

7. **Don't /isn't** worry about that.

8. It **won't/would've** been nice to go on vacation.

APPLY Write the *contraction* for the boldfaced words in each sentence below.

9. **I am** going to Arizona in April. _____

10. **I have** never been to the southwest states.

_____

11. **I will** send you a postcard of the desert.

_____

12. **She is** my best friend. _____

13. I know **he is** coming to visit today.

_____

Add *apostrophes* where they are needed to make contractions. Use proofreading marks.

I couldnt think of anything to write. Were supposed to write a poem for class. It doesnt have to be a long poem. I cant think tonight! Couldnt I write about my life? I could, if it werent so late.

Write the *contraction* for the following words.

14. should not _____

15. he is _____

16. cannot _____

17. have not _____

18. there is _____

Grammar • *Skills Practice 2*

/ōō/ spelled *u, u_e, _ew,* and *_ue*

FOCUS The /ōō/ sound can be spelled with *u, u_e, _ew,* and *_ue.*

PRACTICE Use the words in the box to fill in the blanks.

rumor	stew	utility	cashew	tune
drew	ruin	clue	flute	pursue

Write the words with /ōō/ spelled like *grew.*

1. _____   3. _____

2. _____

Write the words with /ōō/ spelled like *rude.*

4. _____   5. _____

Write the words with /ōō/ spelled like *due.*

6. _____   7. _____

Write the words with /ōō/ spelled like *truth.*

8. _____   10. _____

9. _____

APPLY Replace the underlined letter or letters to create a rhyming word. The new word will have the same spelling pattern for /o͞o/.

11. <u>c</u>lue   + tr   = _____

12. <u>n</u>ew   + ch   = _____

13. <u>b</u>lue   + g   = _____

14. <u>con</u>clude + i   = _____

Read the paragraph. Circle the misspelled words. Write the words correctly on the blanks below.

    Summer begins in the month of Jewn. Lots of nue blossoms appear on trees and plants. People swim in cool, bloo pools. They listen to tewns as they cut the grass. Other summer activities inclood hiking and camping. Some like to brue iced tea and then sip it on the porch.

15. _____

16. _____

17. _____

18. _____

19. _____

20. _____

Prefix *pre-*

FOCUS
- A **prefix** is added to the beginning of a word and changes the meaning of that word.
- The prefix *pre-* means "before in place, time, or order." **Example:** pre + made = premade (made ahead of time)

PRACTICE Add the prefix *pre-* to the base words below. Write the new word on the first line. Then write the meaning of the new word.

Base Word	New Word	New Meaning
1. cooked	_____	_____
2. pay	_____	_____
3. pack	_____	_____
4. game	_____	_____

APPLY Write two sentences using the new words from above.

5. _____

_____

6. _____

_____

Prefix mis-

FOCUS
- A **prefix** is added to the beginning of a word and changes the meaning of that word.
- The prefix *mis-* means "bad," "wrong," or "incorrectly." **Example:** mis + judge = misjudge (to judge incorrectly)

PRACTICE Add the prefix *mis-* to the base words below. Write the new word on the first line. Then write the meaning of the new word.

Base Word	New Word	New Meaning
7. count	_____	_____
8. behave	_____	_____
9. match	_____	_____
10. place	_____	_____

APPLY Fill in the blank with the prefix *pre-* or *mis-* to create a new word that makes sense in the sentence.

11. Kaylee felt like a _____ fit and didn't have fun at camp.

12. Dad _____ arranged for a cab to pick us up at the airport.

13. If you _____ soak the shirt before washing, the stain might come out.

14. Toby would never _____ treat his pets.

Vocabulary

> **FOCUS** Review the vocabulary words from "The Green Grass Grew All Around."

around	**ground**	**root**
branch	**middle**	**twig**
ever		

PRACTICE Synonyms mean the same or nearly the same thing. Circle the vocabulary word that matches the underlined synonym in each sentence below.

1. A belt goes around the <u>center</u> of a person's body.

   a. ever   **b.** middle   **c.** ground

2. There were flowers <u>everywhere</u> in the meadow.

   a. around   **b.** ever   **c.** middle

3. The cherry hung from a tiny <u>stick</u> on a tree limb.

   a. twig   **b.** root   **c.** ground

4. A carrot is actually a <u>tuber</u> that grows underground.

   a. branch   **b.** around   **c.** root

APPLY *Alliteration* happens when several words begin with the same sound. It is something writers use to give stories and poems rhythm. Use a vocabulary word to complete each example of alliteration below.

5. The bulging, broken birch _____ bent beneath her boot.

6. Will Emily _____ enter the egg exhibition?

7. Greg grew grumpy with the gloppy gravel

_____.

8. The mist made the _____ of the maze murky.

9. The running rain reached the rough _____.

10. Asters bloomed all _____ the alley.

Cause and Effect

> **FOCUS**
> - A **cause** is *why* something happens.
> - An **effect** is *what* happens.

PRACTICE Read each sentence. Write the *effect* (what happened) and the *cause* (why it happened).

1. Because the hiker wore new boots, her feet had blisters.

Effect: _____

Cause: _____

2. Because the mother fed her baby bird, the bird grew strong.

Effect: _____

Cause: _____

3. Since the farmer released some ladybugs, there have been fewer aphids harming the crops.

Effect: _____

Cause: _____

4. Because the tree's roots were deep, the tree took in water deep underground.

Effect: _____

Cause: _____

APPLY Read each *cause* from "The Green Grass Grew All Around." Write an *effect* to complete each sentence.

5. Because there was a hole in the ground, _____

_____.

6. Because there was a nest on the twig, _____

_____.

7. Because there was an egg in the nest, _____

_____.

At the end of "The Green Grass Grew All Around," the illustration shows the baby bird growing up. Think about this as a *cause*. Write two *effects*.

8. Because the baby bird grew up, _____ _____

and _____ _____.

Writing to Inform

Think

Audience: *Who* will read your biography?

_____

Purpose: *What* is your reason for writing a biography?

_____

Prewriting

Use this graphic organizer to identify the person who will be the topic of your biography, and list three details from his or her life that your biography will include.

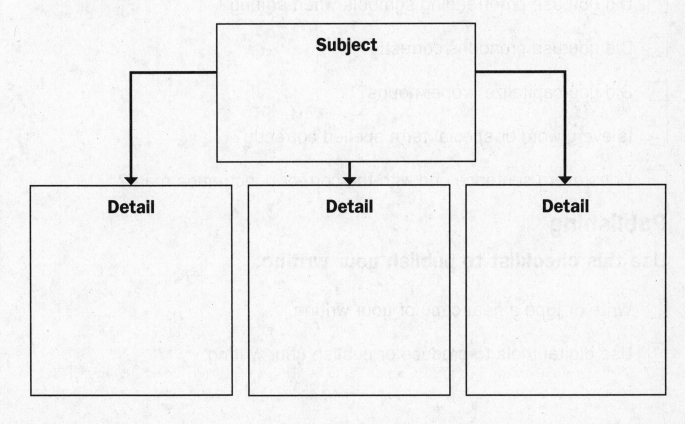

Revising

Use this checklist to revise your writing.

☐ Did you include a topic sentence that clearly introduces the subject of your biography?

☐ Did you include interesting and relevant details from the person's life?

☐ Did you use temporal words?

☐ Did you add details or descriptions that were missing?

☐ Did you include interesting and descriptive details?

☐ Does your writing contain a clear purpose?

Editing/Proofreading

Use this checklist to correct mistakes in your writing.

☐ Did you use proofreading symbols when editing?

☐ Did you use pronouns correctly?

☐ Did you capitalize proper nouns?

☐ Is every word or special term spelled correctly?

☐ Does every sentence end with the correct punctuation mark?

Publishing

Use this checklist to publish your writing.

☐ Write or type a neat copy of your writing.

☐ Use digital tools to produce or publish your writing.

/o͞o/ spelled *u*, *u_e*, *_ew*, and *_ue;* Prefixes *pre-* and *mis-*

FOCUS
- The /o͞o/ sound sounds like the underlined part of the word *n<u>ew</u>*.
- Some ways the /o͞o/ sound can be spelled are *u*, *u_e*, *_ew*, and *_ue*.
- The prefix *pre-* means "before."
- The prefix *mis-* means "bad," "wrong," or "incorrectly."

PRACTICE Sort the spelling words.

/o͞o/ spelled *u*

1. _____

/o͞o/ spelled *u_e*

2. _____

3. _____

/o͞o/ spelled *_ew*

4. _____

5. _____

/o͞o/ spelled *_ue*

6. _____

Words with the prefix *pre-*

7. _____

8. _____

Words with the prefix *mis-*

9. _____

10. _____

Word List
1. clue
2. blew
3. tube
4. misread
5. preheat
6. student
7. grew
8. precut
9. mislead
10. June

Challenge Words
11. blueberry
12. salute
13. misunderstand
14. preview
15. assume

APPLY Write the spelling word next to its meaning clue.

11. already cut   _____

12. read incorrectly   _____

13. used air to move   _____

14. a hint   _____

15. heat before   _____

Circle the correct spelling for each word below. Then write the correct spelling on the line.

16. Joon   June   _____

17. student   stewdunt   _____

18. mislead   missleed   _____

19. tueb   tube   _____

20. groo   grew   _____

Possessive Nouns

> **FOCUS**
> - A **noun** is a person, place, thing, or idea.
> - A **possessive noun** shows ownership.
> - A **plural possessive noun** ends in just an apostrophe s (').
>
> **Examples:**
> **Singular:** *Jennifer's* mother works at the library.
> **Plural:** The *books'* covers were torn.

PRACTICE Write the *possessive* form of the noun in parentheses ( ) on the line.

1. I played with my _____ hamster. (friend)

2. The _____ dresses were green. (girls)

3. _____ brother knows a lot of magic tricks. (Megan)

4. My _____ saddle is brand new. (horse)

5. The _____ suggestion was very helpful. (librarian)

6. _____ dog is a beagle. (Sean)

Possessive Pronouns

FOCUS A **possessive pronoun** takes the place of a possessive noun. There is no apostrophe (') at the end.
Examples:
Singular: *Jennifer's* mother works at the library.
Her mother works at the library.

Plural: The *books'* covers were torn.
Their covers were torn.

PRACTICE Circle the correct *pronoun* to replace the underlined *noun*.

1. <u>Andrew's</u> treasure map was buried in the yard. (He, His)

2. We went to <u>Beth's</u> house after school yesterday. (she, her)

3. <u>The peacock's</u> feathers were very colorful. (Its, You)

4. <u>Jessica's</u> bike is just like mine. (She, Her)

5. I like to listen to <u>Zach's</u> radio. (his, he)

6. <u>My dog's</u> leash is yellow. (Your, Its)

7. <u>Lisa's</u> home is next door to the bank. (Her, She)

8. <u>The windows'</u> locks are broken. (Its, Their)

Ocean Life

Did you know that ocean water has salt in it? Thousands of living things make the ocean their home. Plants and animals have parts that help them live in the saltwater. Some creatures are tiny, but the largest animal on Earth lives in the ocean too!

Kelp is a kind of plant that lives in the ocean. It can grow very tall under water. It is very different from land plants. It does not have a trunk like trees. Kelp is not delicate though. It has strong stems that can move in the water. Parts that trap air bubbles help this plant float. Then it can get closer to the sunlight above the water.

Many kinds of plants live in the ocean. Some plants are large like kelp. Other plants are so tiny that you need a microscope to see them! These tiny plants float in the water. They like to live in cool water. They need a lot of sunlight to live.

The bottom of the ocean does not get much sunlight. It is very dark and cold. One kind of fish that lives there glows like a flashlight! The glowing part helps the fish find food. This part can be bad though. Sometimes it is hard for this fish to hide from other animals.

Living things in Earth's oceans help each other. A sea anemone is an animal that lives in the ocean. It can sting other animals. It does not harm one kind of fish though. The clownfish shares its food with the anemone. A sea anemone is a protective home for the clownfish.

Another ocean animal is a giant octopus. It is big and has eight arms! It is a shy, but very smart animal. An octopus can change the coloration of its body. Then it can blend in with parts of the ocean. The camouflage helps the octopus get food and hide from other animals.

The largest animal on Earth is the blue whale. It eats tiny plants and animals. During the summer, blue whales like to live in cool ocean water. A lot of food can be found there. During the winter, blue whales live in warm ocean water. Baby blue whales are born there.

The ocean is home to many plants and animals. Scientists continue to learn more and more about the ocean every year. You should too!

Vocabulary

FOCUS Review the vocabulary words from "Winston & George."

clattering	prowling	stammered
current	reluctantly	suddenly
demanded	resist	tempted
hovered	shoal	yank
moment	snout	

PRACTICE Circle Yes or No to answer each question below.

1. If a plate made a *clattering* sound, was it a loud rattling noise?

   Yes   No

2. If a girl *stammered*, did she speak clearly?

   Yes   No

3. If children *yank* a rope, do they pull it hard?

   Yes   No

4. If a helicopter *hovered*, did it fly and hang in one place?

   Yes   No

APPLY Circle the correct words to complete the folktale below.

Once Monkey, who lived in an apple tree, befriended Crocodile, who lived nearby on the river **5.** (shoal, yank). Monkey would ride on Crocodile's back as the river's **6.** (shoal, current) pulled them along. Any **7.** (moment, suddenly) that Crocodile asked, Monkey scampered up his tree and picked apples to feed to Crocodile.

Crocodile's wife, who was **8.** (clattering, prowling) quietly one day, saw Monkey. She could not **9.** (stammered, resist) the thought of eating him up. The thought **10.** (tempted, demanded) her day and night. Finally, she **11.** (hovered, demanded) that Crocodile bring her Monkey to gobble up. Crocodile, although he was sad, **12.** (reluctantly, clattering) agreed.

The next time Monkey hopped onto Crocodile's **13.** (snout, shoal) for a ride, Crocodile said, "I am sorry, Monkey, but I have to take you to my wife. She wants to eat you up."

Monkey, thinking fast, **14.** (suddenly, clattering) said, "Okay, Crocodile, but you need to take me to my tree. Monkeys always leave their hearts in trees. I need to go get it so your wife can have it, too."

Crocodile was surprised, but took Monkey back. With one **15.** (yank, hovered) on a tree branch, Monkey swung up high and did not come back. Crocodile left, and his wife had to eat something else for dinner.

Fact and Opinion

> **FOCUS**
> - A *fact* states something that can happen, has happened, or is real. You can do research to check a fact.
> - An *opinion* states something someone <u>believes</u> to have happened or to be true. Words often used in opinions include: *believe*, *think*, *feel*, *always*, *best*, *worst*, and *never*.

PRACTICE Read each sentence below. Circle *Fact* or *Opinion*.

1. A tree is a plant.

   Fact   **Opinion**

2. Jazz is the best kind of music.

   Fact   **Opinion**

3. Everyone should like eating strawberries.

   Fact   **Opinion**

4. Running is a type of exercise.

   Fact   **Opinion**

5. Running is always good for everyone.

   Fact   **Opinion**

APPLY Read the following quotes from
"Winston & George." Decide if they are *fact*
or *opinion*.

6. "A crocodile bird that plays pranks deserves to be eaten up!"

   Fact or **Opinion?** _____

7. "Winston woke up three miles downstream."

   Fact or **Opinion?** _____

8. "And from that day on, George didn't play any more pranks
   on his patient crocodile, although he was tempted to many,
   many times."

   Fact or **Opinion?** _____

9. "It was very funny at first to see a crocodile's feet and tail
   kicking and wagging in the air."

   Fact or **Opinion?** _____

**Choose one of the quotes above. Explain how you
knew it was a *fact* or an *opinion*.**

10. I know quote number _____ above was a

    _____ because _____

    _____.

Access Complex Text • *Skills Practice 2*

/oo/ spelled oo

FOCUS The /oo/ sound is spelled with *oo*. The *oo* spelling pattern is usually found in the middle of a word.

PRACTICE Use the letters in parentheses ( ) to write a word on the line with the *oo* spelling pattern.

1. (b, k) _____

2. (f, t) _____

3. (w, d) _____

4. (h, k) _____

5. (h, d) _____

6. (c, k) _____

7. (s, t, d) _____

8. (s, h, k) _____

9. (l, k) _____

10. (w, l) _____

APPLY Read each word, and then write a new rhyming word on the line.

11. book   _____

12. hood   _____

13. shook   _____

14. look   _____

15. stood   _____

Complete each sentence by writing one of the above words on the blank line.

16. I like to read a _____ before I go to sleep.

17. My jacket has a _____ for cold or rainy weather.

18. Charlie _____ at the bus stop with his friends.

19. The doctor is taking a _____ at Anna's sore throat.

20. The mayor _____ hands with all of her supporters.

Comparative Ending *-er*, Superlative Ending *-est*, and Irregular Comparatives

FOCUS
- The **comparative ending** *-er* shows a comparison between two things.
- The **superlative ending** *-est* shows a comparison among three or more things.
- Some words that show comparison do not follow the usual patterns of adding *-er* or *-est*. These words are **irregular comparatives.**

PRACTICE Add *-er* to the following words. Write each new word on the line.

1. clean _____

3. easy _____

2. mad _____

4. dark _____

Add *-est* to the following words. Write each new word on the line.

5. bright _____

7. smooth _____

6. funny _____

8. wise _____

Draw a line to match the comparative form to its superlative form.

9. worse   **a.** best

10. more   **b.** most

11. less   **c.** worst

12. better   **d.** least

APPLY Circle the correct word to complete each sentence.

13. Lance's bike is (newer, newest) than Henry's.

14. Mr. Jones raked the (biggest, bigger) pile of leaves on our street.

15. The lunchroom is (noisyest, noisiest) on Fridays.

16. Which of these two books costs (less, least)?

17. This feels like the (hottest, hotest) day of the year!

18. Nate's hair is (curlier, curlyer) on rainy days.

19. Kate said that was the (worse, worst) movie she'd ever seen!

20. The public pool is (deepest, deeper) than our swimming pool.

21. The new washer works much (best, better) than the old one did.

22. Zack has the (least, less) amount of absences this year.

23. I thought the sequel was (least, less) exciting than the first movie.

24. The car looked a lot (shiniest, shinier) after we waxed it.

Vocabulary

> **FOCUS** Review the vocabulary words from "A Brand-New American Family."

anticipation	federal	register
charge	gnawed	revolving
courthouse	hints	uphold
faithfully	keen	vendors

PRACTICE Circle the vocabulary word that could replace the underlined word or words in each sentence.

1. The <u>building where courts of law were held</u> was in the center of the city.

    a. vendors   **b.** charge   **c.** courthouse

2. The children <u>chewed over and over</u> on the large pretzels.

    a. gnawed   **b.** uphold   **c.** revolving

3. The family decided to <u>sign up</u> for classes at the recreation center.

    a. register   **b.** uphold   **c.** faithfully

4. The <u>people who sold things</u> had set up stalls all around the fair.

    a. courthouse   **b.** hints   **c.** vendors

APPLY Circle the vocabulary word that completes each sentence below.

5. Today there is much (vendors, anticipation) when a U.S. president is sworn in, but when Thomas Jefferson first did this it was very simple.

6. In 1801, the (revolving, federal) government had only recently moved to Washington, D.C.

7. Jefferson was the first president elect to make the promise to (uphold, revolve) the office there.

8. The half-built buildings only gave (federal, hints) of what the city would become.

9. Only people with a (anticipation, keen) eye would have noticed it—few people came to the ceremony.

10. The Chief Justice (gnawed, charged) Jefferson with his responsibilities.

11. Jefferson promised to (faithfully, federal) do the job, and then went back to the boarding house where he was staying.

12. Today, things are very different; parties and fanfare (revolve, charge) around the inauguration of a president.

Making Inferences

> **FOCUS** When you *make inferences*, you use information provided in a text, along with what you already know, to understand details the author did not put in the story.

PRACTICE Read each group of sentences.
Circle the correct inference.

1. The girl's eyes drooped. She yawned and tipped her head to one side.

   a. The girl was tired.   **b.** The girl was sad.

2. When the boy sipped his drink, he spluttered. Then he held it carefully and blew on it for a couple minutes.

   a. The drink was tasty.   **b.** The drink was hot.

3. There were charred bits of wood in the bottom of the fireplace. Some smoke rose from them.

   a. The fireplace was rarely used.

   b. The fireplace had recently held a fire.

4. The book was battered and worn. The cover was slightly ripped.

   a. The book was old.

   b. The book was not interesting.

APPLY Read each quote from "A Brand-New American Family." Use what you already know to answer each question that follows and make an inference.

Mamá stood and began to gather their trash. "We should go. We don't want to be late for the ceremony."

Ana clapped her hands and jumped off the bench. She twirled around, her skirt flaring out to catch the breeze.

5. What inference can you make about Ana's mood and its cause?

_____

6. What information did you use to make this inference?

_____

Ana repeated each line faithfully, though some of the words were hard for her. Papá smiled down at her and gave her hand an encouraging squeeze.

7. What inference can you make about Ana and her father's relationship?

_____

8. What information did you use to make this inference?

_____

Personal Letter

Think

Audience: *Who* will read your personal letter?

_____

_____

Purpose: *What* is your reason for writing a personal letter?

_____

_____

Prewriting

Use this graphic organizer to plan your personal letter.

1. **Start with the date and the word *Dear*, and then add the person's name.**	
2. **Explain the topic of your letter.**	
3. **Tell details about the topic.**	
4. **Choose a personal closing. It could be *Love*, or *Your friend*.**	

Revising

Use this checklist to revise your writing.

- [ ] Is the topic of your letter clear?

- [ ] Did you add anything that was left out of your letter?

- [ ] Did you use words and phrases that show how you feel about the topic?

- [ ] Did you tell about the things you did?

- [ ] Did you use synonyms to avoid repeated words or phrases?

- [ ] Did you use language that is appropriate for your audience and purpose?

Editing/Proofreading

Use this checklist to correct mistakes in your writing.

- [ ] Did you use commas and capitalization correctly in the greeting and closing?

- [ ] Does every name begin with a capital letter?

- [ ] Is every word or special term spelled correctly?

- [ ] Does each sentence begin with a capital letter and end with the correct punctuation mark?

Publishing

Use this checklist to publish your writing.

- [ ] Write or type a neat copy of your writing.

- [ ] Sign your letter.

- [ ] Address an envelope to mail your letter.

/oo/ spelled *oo;* Comparative Ending *-er;* Superlative Ending *-est;* Irregular Comparatives

FOCUS
- the /oo/ sound is spelled *oo,* as in the word *cook.*
- The **comparative ending** *-er* shows a comparison between two things. The ending *-er* is usually added to a base word.
- The **superlative ending** *-est* shows a comparison between three or more things. The ending *-est* is usually added to a base word.
- **Irregular comparatives** do not follow these rules.

PRACTICE Sort the spelling words.

/oo/ spelled *oo*

1. _____
2. _____
3. _____
4. _____
5. _____
6. _____

Comparative with *-er* added to base word

7. _____

Superlative with *-est* added to base word

8. _____

Irregular Comparatives

9. _____
10. _____

Word List		Challenge Words
1. look	**6.** hotter	**11.** worst
2. good	**7.** brook	**12.** childhood
3. shook	**8.** hoof	**13.** bookmark
4. stood	**9.** better	**14.** uncooked
5. highest	**10.** least	**15.** happier

APPLY

Choose the correct spelling for each word. Then pronounce each word carefully, and write it on the line.

11. look   luk   _____

12. hiust   highest   _____

13. stuud   stood   _____

14. hufe   hoof   _____

15. shook   shuk   _____

Replace the underlined letter in each word with a new letter to form a spelling word.

16. <u>c</u>ook + br = _____

17. <u>h</u>ood + g = _____

18. <u>bl</u>otter + h = _____

19. <u>l</u>etter + b = _____

20. <u>be</u>ast + l = _____

Capitals and Commas in Letter Greetings/Closings

FOCUS
- The beginning of a friendly letter is called the *greeting* or *salutation*.
- The first word begins with a capital letter.
- A comma is written after the name in the greeting.
  Example: Dear John,
- The end of a friendly letter is called the *closing.*
- The first word begins with a capital letter.
- A comma is written after the closing.
- The sender's name is written beneath the closing.
  Example: Love,
           Alice

PRACTICE Rewrite the greetings and closings correctly. Insert commas and capitalize letters when needed.

1. dear oscar   _____

2. respectfully   _____

   Jayce   _____

3. best wishes   _____

   Isabella   _____

4. my dear nina   _____

APPLY Add capital letters and commas where they are needed. Use the following proofreading marks: ⌄ to insert a comma and ≡ beneath the letters that need to be capitalized.

March 16, 2015

dear liam

    I am glad to have a brave friend like you. You were not afraid to stand up for me when joe was teasing me. I tried not to care, but he was hurting my feelings. i will try to do the same thing for you in the future. I also like to play video games and ride bikes with you. Playing the fantastic flyers game is also great. you are my best friend!

                    sincerely

                    caden

/ow/ spelled ow and *ou_*

FOCUS The /ow/ sound can be spelled ow and *ou_*.

PRACTICE **Read the sentence. Change the word in the box to make a new rhyming word that completes the sentence. Write the new word on the line.**

1. | brown | The queen's _____ is made of solid gold and real jewels.

2. | found | Worms and other animals live beneath the _____.

3. | couch | A baby kangaroo travels in its mother's _____.

4. | town | The _____ on Eric's face told us he was quite unhappy.

5. | chowder | Suki sprinkles _____ in her boots to keep her feet dry.

6. | sound | We bake pies in a _____ pan and cakes in a rectangular pan.

APPLY Read the sentence. Circle the word that completes each sentence. Write the word on the line.

7. Use a hammer to _____ the nails into the wood.

   a. pownd   **b.** pound   **c.** pond   **d.** puond

8. The _____ cheered when our team won the game.

   a. crowd   **b.** crowed   **c.** croud   **d.** croued

9. Who gets to take a _____ first this morning?

   a. shouwer   **b.** shour   **c.** shouer   **d.** shower

10. Liza wore a new _____ and skirt to the meeting.

    a. blouse   **b.** blows   **c.** blues   **d.** blous

Read each hint. Fill in the blank with *ow* or *ou* to complete the word.

11. squeaks and eats cheese   m_____se

12. has a petals and a stem   fl_____er

13. used for drying off   t_____el

14. used for eating and talking   m_____th

15. what basketballs do   b_____nce

16. sound a wolf makes   h_____l

Suffixes *-er, -or,* and *-ness*

FOCUS
- A **suffix** is added to the end of a base word. Adding a suffix changes the meaning of the word.
- The suffixes *-er* and *-or* can mean "one who." They refer to a person or thing that does a certain action.
  Examples: heat + er = heater (a thing that heats) collect + or = collector (one who collects)
- The suffix *-ness* means "the state of being."
  Example: dark + ness = darkness (the state of being dark)

PRACTICE Add the suffix *-er, -or,* or *-ness* to the base words below. Write the new word, and then write its meaning.

	New Word	Meaning
1. work + er =	_____	_____
2. calculate + or =	_____	_____
3. still + ness =	_____	_____
4. act + or =	_____	_____
5. goofy + ness =	_____	_____
6. manage + er =	_____	_____

APPLY Add the suffix *-er, -or,* or *-ness* to a word from the box. Then write the word to complete a sentence.

ill	play	sail	dance
love	bright	illustrate	silly

7. Dr. Burns will know how to cure the _____.

8. She is the author and the _____ of the book.

9. Wear sunglasses to shield your eyes from the _____ of the sun.

10. The _____ moved on stage with rhythm and grace.

11. Children giggled at the clown's _____.

12. Did the _____ send a message from her boat?

13. Which hockey _____ scored the goal?

14. Lee is an animal _____ and has lots of pets.

Write two sentences using the words in the box below.

dreamer	shyness	protector

15. _____

_____

16. _____

_____

Vocabulary

> **FOCUS** Review the vocabulary words from "United States Citizenship."

citizen	legally	rights
democracy	naturalized	symbol
emigrated	oath	traits
immigrated	republic	voice

PRACTICE Match each vocabulary word with its definition below.

1. republic

a. born in another country but becomes a citizen

2. democracy

b. a promise a person makes

3. traits

c. qualities of a person or animal

4. citizen

d. allowed by the law

5. naturalized

e. to leave one's own country and live in another

6. legally

f. a government run by the people who live under it

7. oath

g. a member of a country

8. emigrated

h. government where people elect leaders

APPLY Use a vocabulary word to complete each sentence below. Use context clues to help you.

9. In the 1800s, many Europeans left their native countries and _____ to the United States.

10. These people _____ here for many reasons.

11. Many longed to have a _____ and be heard by a government.

Homophones are words that sound alike but have different spellings and meanings. Choose the homophone that completes each sentence below.

cymbal	symbol	rights	writes

12. The teacher _____ a math problem on the board.

13. American women did not have voting _____ for many years.

14. The Statue of Liberty is a _____ of freedom.

15. The drum player hit the _____ with a loud crash.

Main Idea and Details

FOCUS
- The *main idea* tells what a paragraph is about. It is the most important idea presented by the author.
- *Details* provide specific information about the *main idea*.

PRACTICE Each paragraph below is missing a main idea sentence. Circle the main idea that goes with each group of details.

1. Marie goes for a run three times a week. She also takes several kinds of dance classes.

   a. Marie is very athletic.

   b. Marie lives in New York City.

2. Good citizens help their neighbors even when it is not convenient. They take the time to learn about issues when deciding how to vote.

   a. Good citizens live everywhere.

   b. Good citizens must work hard.

APPLY Think about "United States Citizenship." Look at each group of details below. Write a main idea that could go with the details to form a paragraph.

3. **Main Idea:** _____

   Details: Immigrants coming to Ellis Island were tired and sick. They often had traveled a long way.

4. **Main Idea:** _____

   Details: Citizens have freedom of speech. Citizens can practice any religion they choose. Citizens also have the right to vote.

Think about "A Brand-New American Family" and "United States Citizenship." Look at the main idea below. Use information from both selections to write two details to go with it.

   Main Idea: When an immigrant becomes a U.S. citizen, there is a ceremony.

5. _____

   _____

6. _____

   _____

Access Complex Text • *Skills Practice 2*

Response to Literature

Think

Audience: *Who* will read your response to literature?

_____

Purpose: *What* is your reason for writing a response to literature?

_____

Prewriting

Identify three details about the main character in "A Brand-New American Family."

Main Character: _____

Detail 1: _____

_____

Detail 2: _____

_____

Detail 3: _____

_____

Revising

Use this checklist to revise your writing.

☐ Did you identify the main character in the story?

☐ Did you use temporal words to describe events that happen to the character?

☐ Did you include details describing the character's feelings and actions?

☐ Did you use language that is appropriate for your audience and purpose?

☐ Is your purpose for writing clear?

Editing/Proofreading

Use this checklist to correct mistakes in your writing.

☐ Did you use quotation marks around any phrases that were taken directly from the story?

☐ Does every name begin with a capital letter?

☐ Is every word spelled correctly?

☐ Does each sentence begin with a capital letter and end with the correct punctuation mark?

Publishing

Use this checklist to publish your writing.

☐ Write or type a neat copy of your writing.

☐ Include an illustration of the character.

/ow/ spelled *ow* and *ou_*; Suffixes *-er, -or,* and *-ness*

FOCUS
- The /ow/ sound sounds like the word *cow* or *out*. Two ways it can be spelled are *ow* and *ou_*.
- The suffixes *-er* and *-or* mean "one who." When they are added to base words, they change the base words' meanings.
- The suffix *-ness* means "the state of being." When it is added to a base word, it changes the base word's meaning.

PRACTICE Sort the spelling words.

/ow/ spelled *ow*

1. _____

2. _____

3. _____

/ow/ spelled *ou_*

4. _____

5. _____

Suffix *-er*

6. _____

7. _____

Suffix *-or*

8. _____

Suffix *-ness*

9. _____

10. _____

Word List		Challenge Words
1. teacher	**6.** town	**11.** collector
2. hour	**7.** howl	**12.** outside
3. loud	**8.** baker	**13.** powder
4. kindness	**9.** actor	**14.** laziness
5. crowd	**10.** brightness	**15.** shower

APPLY

Write the spelling word or words that rhyme with each word below.

11. proud _____ _____

12. power _____

13. prowl _____

14. down _____

15. maker _____

Circle the correct spelling for the following words. Then write the correctly spelled word on the line.

16. acter   actor   _____

17. brightness   briteniss   _____

18. kindness   kinedniss   _____

Verb Tenses

FOCUS
- Finding the right verb and using the right tense of the verb is important when speaking and writing.
- A **present-tense** verb tells about something that is happening right now.

  Example: I *walk* to school.
- A **past-tense** verb tells about something that happened in the past.

  Example: I *walked* to school yesterday.
- A **future-tense** verb tells about something that will happen in the future.

  Example: I *will* walk to school tomorrow.
- Some verbs do not add *-ed* to change from present to past tense. They change in other ways.

  Example: I *sing*. I *sang*.

PRACTICE Write the past and future tense for each verb on the lines.

Present Tense	Past Tense	Future Tense
1. look	_____	_____
2. grow	_____	_____
3. drive	_____	_____

APPLY Complete each sentence with the correct tense of the boldfaced verb.

4. I **gave** today. Next week I will _____.

5. Yesterday they **bought** food. Today they will _____ food.

6. We **are** happy. Last week we _____ happy.

7. Last month I **sang.** Tomorrow I will _____.

8. I can **throw** the ball. Yesterday I _____ the ball.

Write the correct verb tense to replace the underlined verb.

9. I will <u>sang</u> loudly at choir practice. _____

10. Tomorrow Ann will <u>rode</u> with us to school. _____

11. When it snowed, our cat <u>come</u> inside. _____

12. Yesterday, there <u>is</u> nowhere to play. _____

13. Next year I will <u>am</u> in third grade. _____

14. Make sure to <u>looked</u> for cars before crossing the street. _____

Name _____ **Date** _____

/oo/ and /ow/

FOCUS
- The /oo/ sound is spelled oo.
- The /ow/ sound can be spelled ow or ou_.

PRACTICE Sort the words under the correct heading.

hook	frown	stood	pout
amount	woof	prowl	council

/oo/ spelled oo

1. _____

2. _____

3. _____

/ow/ spelled ow

4. _____

5. _____

/ow/ spelled ou_

6. _____

7. _____

8. _____

Copyright © McGraw-Hill Education

APPLY Use a word from the box to complete each sentence.

scowl	pouch	cookies	plow	round
hoof	drown	cloud	look	flour

9. Layne keeps her pencils in a zippered _____.

10. Oranges and apples are both _____.

11. A large tractor pulls the _____ across the field.

12. There wasn't a _____ in the clear, blue sky.

13. Sally likes to drink milk with her _____.

14. The grumpy store clerk always has a _____ on his face.

15. Mix milk, butter, and _____ to make the batter.

16. The goat's _____ was covered in mud.

17. Manny likes to _____ his pancakes in syrup.

18. Never _____ directly at the sun!

Suffixes -*ly* and -*y*

FOCUS
- A **suffix** is added to the end of a base word. Adding a suffix changes the meaning of the word.
- The suffix -*ly* means "in a certain way."
- The suffix -*y* means "like" or "full of."

PRACTICE Choose a suffix from above to add to each base word. Write the meaning of the new word.

1. quick _____ Meaning: _____

2. fur _____ Meaning: _____

3. thirst _____ Meaning: _____

4. loud _____ Meaning: _____

Write three sentences using the words from above.

5. _____

_____

6. _____

_____

7. _____

_____

APPLY Add *-ly* or *-y* to the base word in parentheses ( )
to form a new word that completes the sentence.
Write the new word on the line. Then write the meaning
of the new word.

8. (Storm) _____ weather makes our pets upset.

New Meaning: _____

9. Spread the butter (even) _____ on the toast.

New Meaning: _____

10. A bird (sudden) _____ flew into the window.

New Meaning: _____

11. We need to clean out our (mess) _____
basement this weekend.

New Meaning: _____

12. Hold the baby chick very (careful) _____ .

New Meaning: _____

13. Liza (bold) _____ stepped up to the microphone.

New Meaning: _____

14. The spilled glue left a (stick) _____ spot on
my desk.

New Meaning: _____

15. Trevor trimmed the dog's (shag) _____ fur.

New Meaning: _____

Word Analysis • *Skills Practice 2*

Vocabulary

> **FOCUS** Review the vocabulary words from "The Flag
> We Love."

allegiance	**ideals**	**solemn**
connotations	**patriots**	**weary**
diligent	**righteous**	

PRACTICE Circle the vocabulary word that best
completes each sentence below.

1. The people's fight against the evil ruler was a _____
cause.

    a. righteous   **b.** connotations   **c.** patriots

2. Because the ceremony was a _____ time, no one
laughed.

    a. ideals   **b.** diligent   **c.** solemn

3. The knights pledged _____ to the king when they
swore to follow him.

    a. righteous   **b.** ideals   **c.** allegiance

4. The _____ children could not walk another step.

    a. ideals   **b.** solemn   **c.** weary

APPLY Words can have *connotations*. Explain what *connotations* are, based on what you know about that word's meaning.

5. _____

Read each group of sentences and think about the connotation of the underlined word or words. Use it to answer the question.

6. During the War for Independence, people in the United States fought for freedom from England. The people here called themselves <u>patriots</u>. What kind of connotation does the word *patriots* have?

_____

_____

7. The people in England, on the other hand, called these same people <u>rebels</u>. Rebels are people who fight the rightful government. What connotation does the word *rebels* have, as opposed to *patriots*?

_____

_____

8. A teacher calls Moses a <u>diligent</u> worker. The teacher says he has high <u>ideals</u>. Does the teacher think well of Moses as a student? Why or why not?

_____

Making Inferences

> **FOCUS** When you *make inferences*, you use information provided in a text, along with what you already know, to understand details the author did not put in the story.

PRACTICE Read the description of each person below. Make an inference about how the person feels.

1. Danny did not look at anyone when he stood in front of the microphone. He spoke very softly. Then he quickly sat down.

   I infer that Danny feels _____ because _____

   _____ .

2. Ebony laughed and jumped up and down.

   I infer that Ebony feels _____ because _____

   _____ .

3. Mr. Gonzalez rubbed his eyes. He sank down in a chair.

   I infer that Mr. Gonzalez feels _____ because

   _____ .

4. Ming threw down her papers and slammed the door.

   I infer that Ming feels _____ because _____

   _____ .

APPLY Read each quote from "The Flag We Love."
Use what you already know to make an inference.
Explain your answers.

"A seamstress stitched a banner
For a country proud and new
From ribbonworks of red and white
And a yard of deep sky blue."

5. What inference can you make about the time and person this

   text is talking about? _____

6. What information from the text helped you? What did you

   already know that helped you? _____

   _____

   _____

"Astronauts planted a peaceful flag
On a far-off, distant world . . ."

7. What inference can you make about why American astronauts

   planted the flag? _____

8. What information did you use to make this inference?

   _____

Formal Letter

Think

Audience: *Who* will read your formal letter?

_____

Purpose: *What* is your reason for writing a formal letter?

_____

Prewriting

Use this graphic organizer to plan your formal letter.

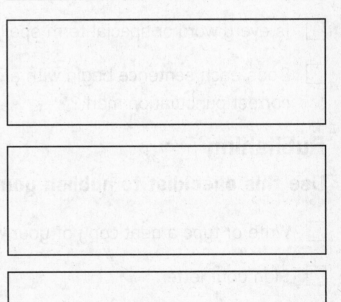

1. Heading: Start with your name and address. Then add the date.	
2. Inside Address: Add the name and address of the person to whom you are writing.	
3. Greeting: Start with the words *To Whom It May Concern*, or *Dear*, and then add the person's name.	
4. Body: Make a request.	
5. Closing: End your letter with *Thank you*, or *Sincerely*, and then sign your name.	

Revising

Use this checklist to revise your writing.

☐ Is the reason for writing your letter clear?

☐ Did you make a request?

☐ Did you use precise words, so the recipient clearly understands your request?

☐ Did you use formal language?

☐ Is your letter polite?

Editing/Proofreading

Use this checklist to correct mistakes in your writing.

☐ Did you use correct verb tenses?

☐ Does every name begin with a capital letter?

☐ Is every word or special term spelled correctly?

☐ Does each sentence begin with a capital letter and end with the correct punctuation mark?

Publishing

Use this checklist to publish your writing.

☐ Write or type a neat copy of your writing.

☐ Sign your letter.

☐ Address an envelope to mail your letter.

/oo/ spelled *oo*; /ow/ spelled *ow, ou_;* Homophones; Suffixes *-ly* and *-y*

FOCUS
- The sound /oo/ can be spelled *oo*.
- The sound /ow/ can be spelled *ow* and *ou_*.
- Homophones are words that sound the same, but have different spellings and meanings.
- The suffix *-ly* means "in a certain way."
- The suffix *-y* means "full of"

PRACTICE Sort the spelling words.

/oo/ spelled *oo*

1. _____

/ow/ spelled *ow*

2. _____

/ow/ spelled *ou_*

3. _____

Homophones

4. _____

5. _____

Suffix *-ly*

6. _____

7. _____

8. _____

Suffixes *-y*

9. _____

10. _____

Word List
1. foot
2. windy
3. lightly
4. plow
5. quickly
6. cents
7. sense
8. sound
9. itchy
10. bravely

Challenge Words
11. birdhouse
12. easily
13. scowl
14. chowder
15. thirsty

APPLY

Write the spelling word on the line that matches the meaning.

11. full of itching _____

12. in a brave way _____

13. in a quick way _____

14. full of wind _____

15. another word for *pennies* _____

16. touch, taste, or sight _____

Circle the correct spelling for each word. Write the correct spelling on the line.

17. sowned   sound _____

18. fut   foot _____

19. lightly   litely _____

20. plou   plow _____

Prepositions and Prepositional Phrases

FOCUS
- A **preposition** relates a noun or a pronoun to another word or words in a sentence.
- Some prepositions relate direction or place (*on*, *under*, *through*). Others relate time (*after*, *before*, *until*).
- A **prepositional phrase** contains the preposition, its object, and sometimes and article and/or an adjective (*outside the window*, *at six o'clock*)

PRACTICE Circle the preposition in each sentence.

1. The park is near my house.

2. Beside Danita there was a crayon.

3. The soccer game is after school tomorrow.

4. The rabbit ran down the hill quickly.

5. Curtis and Mia drew on the sidewalk.

APPLY Circle the preposition, and underline the prepositional phrase in each sentence.

6. Leaves fell from the maple tree.

7. After dinner we will open our gifts.

8. The new flowers were planted beside the garden fence.

9. Tyler put his gloves in his pocket.

10. Ali will go to the store tomorrow morning.

Write a sentence using the preposition in parentheses.

11. (under) _____

_____

12. (from) _____

_____

13. (before) _____

_____

14. (in) _____

_____

/aw/ spelled *aw*, *au_*, *augh*, *ough*, *all*, and *al*

> **FOCUS** The /aw/ sound can be spelled *aw*, *au_*, *augh*, *ough*, *all*, and *al*.

PRACTICE Sort the words under the correct heading.

flaw	cause	brought	naughty	stalk	awning
recall	haunt	laundry	gnaw	false	stall

/aw/ spelled *aw*

1. _____

2. _____

3. _____

/aw/ spelled *au_*

4. _____

5. _____

6. _____

/aw/ spelled *augh*

7. _____

/aw/ spelled *ough*

8. _____

/aw/ spelled *all*

9. _____

10. _____

/aw/ spelled *al*

11. _____

12. _____

APPLY Use the letters in parentheses and an /aw/ spelling pattern to make a word.

13. (f, t) _____

14. (k, w) _____

15. (h, r, t, o) _____

16. (d, e, r, t) _____

17. (s, b, e, a, b) _____

18. (n, r, d) _____

Circle the correct spelling for each set of words.

19. walet   wallet

20. tought   taught

21. fawlt   fault

22. calm   caulm

23. auful   awful

24. thoughtful   thaughtful

Suffixes *-able* and *-ment*

FOCUS
- A **suffix** is added to the end of a base word. Adding a suffix changes the meaning of the word.
- The suffix *-able* means "able to be or worthy of being" or "tending toward."
- The suffix *-ment* means "the act, process, or result of" or "the condition of being."

PRACTICE **Add the suffix *-able* or *-ment* to the base words below. Write the new word and the meaning of the new word.**

Base Word	*-able*	New Meaning
1. honor	_____	_____
2. use	_____	_____
3. remark	_____	_____

Base Word	*-ment*	New Meaning
4. pay	_____	_____
5. manage	_____	_____
6. excite	_____	_____

APPLY Add the suffix *-able* or *-ment* to a word from the box. Then write the word to complete a sentence.

agree	move	engage
advertise	depend	reason

7. We went to the store after we saw the _____.

8. Even a slight _____ causes pain in Rachel's broken leg.

9. Matt and his parents reached an _____ about his allowance.

10. Is 7:00 a _____ time for the party to start?

11. Riku is a _____ worker who shows up on time every day.

12. The happy couple announced their _____ at the party.

Write two sentences using words from the box.

lovable	valuable	judgment	treatment

13. _____

_____

14. _____

_____

Word Analysis • *Skills Practice 2*

Vocabulary

> **FOCUS** Review the vocabulary words from "I Pledge Allegiance."

bond	**pledge**
efficiently	**refers**
indivisible	**represent**
justice	**values**

PRACTICE Match each word with a phrase that it describes.

1. efficiently

a. a country that cannot be divided

2. indivisible

b. fair treatment for all people

3. bond

c. a promise to be faithful

4. justice

d. done in a quick amount of time

5. pledge

e. a tie that holds people together

6. values

f. people's beliefs about the importance of equality

APPLY **Circle the vocabulary word that completes each sentence.**

7. You might think that the U.S. Constitution's framers came up with all of its ideas. The framers, however, (pledged, referred) to ideas created by the Iroquois Confederacy.

8. The Iroquois Confederacy is a group of Native American nations, or tribes. It (refers, represents) a very old democracy.

9. The Iroquois Confederacy had three main principles: peace, the power of experienced minds, and (bond, justice), or fairness.

10. Five nations agreed to these (bond, values) hundreds of years ago, and then another nation joined the Confederacy a little later.

11. These nations made a (pledge, justice) to support each other, but they also could make some of their own decisions.

12. The (bond, justice) of peace that they shared continues among the Iroquois to this day.

Sequence

FOCUS • *Sequence* is the order in which events in a story occur. Writers often use time and order words to help readers understand the sequence of events.
• *Time* words (*winter, 1900, minutes*) show the passage of time.
• *Order* words (*first, next, later*) show the order in which events happen.

PRACTICE **Read this paragraph carefully. Write the time and order words on the lines below.**

Francis Bellamy wrote the first version of the Pledge of Allegiance in the summer of 1892. He sat down and wrote it in about two hours. Later, people made changes to Bellamy's original pledge. Congress adopted the Pledge of Allegiance in 1942.

Time words	**Order words**
1. _____	5. _____
2. _____	6. _____
3. _____	
4. _____	

APPLY Think about "I Pledge Allegiance." Use what you know from the text to answer the sequence questions below.

7. Based on the information on page 247, what is the first thing the pledge begins with? _____

Based on the information on page 251, what are the last two things the pledge says our nation offers its citizens?

8. _____

9. _____

On pages 252 through 254, "I Pledge Allegiance" gives ways we can show respect to our country. List these four actions. Put them in the order in which they occur in the text.

10. First, we can _____.

11. Next, we can _____.

12. Next, we can _____.

13. Finally, we can _____.

Do you think the sequence of these items is important? Why or why not?

14. _____

_____

126 UNIT 5 • Lesson 4   Access Complex Text • *Skills Practice 2*

Copyright © McGraw-Hill Education

Writing a Summary

Think

Audience: *Who* will read your summary?

_____

Purpose: *What* is your reason for writing a summary?

_____

Prewriting

Use the graphic organizer to organize the notes for your summary.

Topic:

Subtopic:	Subtopic:	Subtopic:

Conclusion:

Revising

Use this checklist to revise your writing.

☐ Did you tell the main ideas and include additional details?

☐ Did you use your own words?

☐ Did you use linking words to organize the details in your summary?

☐ Did you present a neutral point of view in the summary?

☐ Did you use formal language?

Editing/Proofreading

Use this checklist to correct mistakes in your writing.

☐ Did you use prepositions and prepositional phrases correctly?

☐ Are all of your sentences complete?

☐ Is every word or special term spelled correctly?

☐ Does each sentence begin with a capital letter and end with the correct punctuation mark?

Publishing

Use this checklist to publish your writing.

☐ Write or type a neat copy of your writing.

☐ Include a photograph or drawing.

/aw/ spelled aw, au_, augh, ough, all, al; Suffixes -able and -ment

FOCUS
- The sound /aw/ can be spelled *aw, au_, augh, ough, all,* and *al.*
- The suffix *-able* means "capable of or suited for." When the suffix is added to a base word, it changes the meaning.
- The suffix *-ment* means "the action or process of doing something." When the suffix is added to a base word, it changes the meaning.

PRACTICE Sort the spelling words.

/aw/ spelled *aw*

1. _____

/aw/ spelled *ough*

4. _____

Suffix *-able*

7. _____

/aw/ spelled *au_*

2. _____

/aw/ spelled *all*

5. _____

Suffix *-ment*

8. _____

/aw/ spelled *augh*

3. _____

/aw/ spelled *al*

6. _____

9. _____

10. _____

Word List
1. argument
2. hawk
3. sauce
4. payment
5. walk
6. bought
7. caught
8. treatment
9. small
10. lovable

Challenge Words
11. movement
12. daughter
13. thought
14. chalk
15. enjoyable

APPLY

Use the meaning clue to write the correct spelling word on each line.

11. the process of treating _____

12. the action of arguing _____

13. a kind of large bird _____

14. capable of being loved _____

15. the action of paying _____

Circle the correct spelling for each spelling word.
Write the correct spelling on the line.

16. cawt   caught   _____

17. walk   wauk   _____

18. small   smawl   _____

19. sauce   sauss   _____

20. bot   bought   _____

Conjunctions

> **FOCUS** A **conjunction** is a word that connects words or ideas. *And, or,* and *but* are conjunctions.
> **Example:** Rosa walked to the mailbox **and** mailed the letter.

PRACTICE Circle the conjunction in each sentence.

1. Mike and Joe went to camp.

2. Mike went to camp in San Diego, but Joe went to camp in Colorado.

3. The boys swam in the lake and rode horses.

4. Was the best part of camp telling stories by the fire or hiking through the woods?

5. During the summer my favorite activities are rafting and running.

6. My family likes to go camping, but Joe's family likes to go to the beach.

7. In the woods, I saw deer, squirrels, and lots of birds.

APPLY Read the sentences. Write a conjunction (*and, or, but*) on the blank line to complete each sentence.

8. We may skip to school, _____ we will not be late.

9. Marta will buy a birthday card, _____ she may make a card instead.

10. I am wearing a blue cap, _____ I am wearing a blue jacket today.

11. My teacher said it might rain tomorrow, _____ we are still going on our class field trip.

12. The cat loves to play with yarn, _____ she also plays with a ball.

13. Joe will read a book about cars, _____ he may read about dinosaurs.

Use the conjunction in parentheses ( ) to write your own sentence.

14. (and) _____

_____

15. (but) _____

_____

16. (or) _____

_____

/oi/ spelled *oi* and *_oy*

> **FOCUS** The /oi/ sound can be spelled with *oi* and *_oy*.

PRACTICE Write a letter on the line to create a word with the /oy/ spelling pattern. Then write the whole word.

1. _____oy   _____

2. _____oy   _____

3. _____oy   _____

4. _____oy   _____

Write a letter on the lines to create a word with the /oi/ spelling pattern. Then write the whole word.

5. _____oi_____   _____

6. _____oi_____   _____

7. _____oi_____   _____

8. _____oi_____   _____

9. _____oi_____   _____

10. _____oi_____   _____

APPLY Write *oi* or *oy* on the line to complete each word with the correct /oi/ spelling pattern.

11. Juan could not av_____d stepping in the puddle.

12. Lots of girls and b_____s ran around the playground during recess.

13. P_____nt the telescope toward the stars.

14. Rain sp_____led our plans for a picnic.

15. Eliza enj_____s knitting and other crafts.

16. The cake was m_____st and tasty.

17. The r_____al family lives in a palace.

18. A tornado can destr_____ a house in seconds.

19. Please keep your v_____ces down while you are in the library.

20. The c_____ns in Luke's pocket equal 75 cents.

21. Grace is ann_____ed by the ticking clock.

22. Our next v_____age will be a trip to Ireland.

Words with the Same Base

> **FOCUS** A **base word** is a word that can stand alone. A base word can give a clue to the meaning of other words in its **word family.**
> **Example:** base word—kind
> word family—unkind, kindly, kindness, kindest

PRACTICE Write the base word for each word family below.

1. walks, walker, walkway

    base word: _____

2. handed, handful, handy

    base word: _____

3. restate, stately, statement

    base word: _____

4. writer, written, writing

    base word: _____

5. disfavor, favorable, favorite

    base word: _____

APPLY Circle the words in the same word family.
Then write the base word on the line.

6. angles   dangled   triangle

base word: _____

7. judgment   misjudge   juggler

base word: _____

8. refund   funny   funding

base word: _____

9. generous   gently   gentlemen

base word: _____

10. hurried   unhurt   hurtful

base word: _____

11. director   predictor   indirectly

base word: _____

12. unreal   reality   leery

base word: _____

Vocabulary

> **FOCUS** Review the vocabulary words from
> "D Is for Democracy."

committees	judicial	movement
convention	jury	organize
express	liberties	politicians
inauguration	mint	strife

PRACTICE Circle *yes* or *no* to answer each question below.

1. Would *judicial committees* do work that has to do with the law?

    Yes   **No**

2. Could *politicians* go to a convention?

    Yes   **No**

3. Are *liberties* places where books are kept?

    Yes   **No**

4. After people vote for leader, does an *inauguration* mean the leader has been chosen?

    Yes   **No**

5. If there is peace after an election, is this a kind of *strife*?

    Yes   **No**

APPLY Read the definitions for each multiple-meaning word below. Write the number of the definition that matches the example sentence.

express: 1. to say or show a thought. **2.** to squeeze out a liquid.

6. _____ The juicer can <u>express</u> all the juice from the orange.

mint: 1. a place where money is made. **2.** a sweet-smelling plant.

7. _____ The <u>mint</u> prints the country's bills.

movement: 1. the act of changing place. **2.** a group of people working together.

8. _____ The people formed a <u>movement</u> that worked for peace.

organize: 1. to put into order. **2.** to coordinate an event or activity.

9. _____ The woman decided to <u>organize</u> her cupboards.

jury: 1. to judge an art or craft show. **2.** a group of people who hear the facts in a court of law.

10. _____ The <u>jury</u> listened to the lawyers present the case's facts.

Fact and Opinion

> **FOCUS**
> - A *fact* states something that can happen, has happened, or is real. You can do research to check a fact.
> - An *opinion* states something someone <u>believes</u> to have happened or to be true. Words often used in opinions include: *believe, think, feel, always, best, worst,* and *never.*

PRACTICE Read each sentence below. Circle *Fact* or *Opinion*.

1. Summer is the best season.

    Fact   **Opinion**

2. The moon goes around Earth.

    Fact   **Opinion**

3. Everyone should always eat a big breakfast.

    Fact   **Opinion**

4. The concert was wonderful.

    Fact   **Opinion**

5. The Declaration of Independence was adopted in 1776.

    Fact   **Opinion**

APPLY Read the following quotes from "D Is for Democracy." Decide if the underlined words are fact or opinion.

6. "**F** is for Founding Fathers <u>who went to a convention</u>."

   Fact or Opinion? _____

7. "**L** is for First Lad the other White House resident. <u>With a fascinating job</u> and married to the president."

   Fact or Opinion? _____

8. "**N** is for our Nation's capital—Where <u>everyone agrees it's delightful</u> to behold the famous cherry trees."

   Fact or Opinion? _____

9. "**T** is for the Taxes: no longer fees for kings, <u>now our money helps to pay for a thousand different things</u>."

   Fact or Opinion? _____

Choose one of the quotes above. Explain how you knew it was a fact or an opinion.

10. I know quote number _____

    above was a(n) _____ because

    _____.

Narrative Writing

Think

Audience: *Who* will read your story?

_____

Purpose: *What* is your reason for writing your story?

_____

Prewriting

Use the story map below to plan how events will
unfold in your story.

Plot (What Happens)

Beginning: (Problem)	Middle: (Events)	Ending: (How the Problem Is Solved)

Revising

Use this checklist to revise your writing.

☐ Do you clearly describe when and where the story takes place?

☐ Does your plot have a beginning, middle, and ending?

☐ Did you include descriptive adjectives and adverbs?

☐ Is it clear what kind of narrative story you are writing?

Editing/Proofreading

Use this checklist to correct mistakes in your writing.

☐ Did you use proofreading symbols when editing?

☐ Did you indent each new paragraph?

☐ Did you use quotation marks and commas correctly for dialogue?

☐ Does your story use a consistent point of view?

☐ Did you check your writing for spelling mistakes?

Publishing

Use this checklist to publish your writing.

☐ Write or type a neat copy of your writing.

☐ Add a drawing or other illustration.

/oi/ spelled *oi* and _*oy*; Words with the Same Base

> ## *FOCUS*
> - The /oi/ sound can be spelled *oi* and _*oy*.
> - A **base word** is a word that can stand alone. A word family is a group of words that share the same base word.

PRACTICE Sort the spelling words.

/oi/ spelled *oi*

1. _____

2. _____

3. _____

/oi/ spelled _*oy*

4. _____

5. _____

Words with the base word *walk*

6. _____

7. _____

8. _____

Words with the base word *place*

9. _____

10. _____

Word List		Challenge Words
1. join	6. enjoy	11. royal
2. walked	7. sidewalk	12. placement
3. spoil	8. placed	13. moist
4. choice	9. boys	14. rejoice
5. walking	10. replace	15. oyster

APPLY

Write the spelling word that rhymes with each word below. The spelling word will have the same /oi/ spelling pattern as the rhyming word.

11. toys   _____

12. rejoice   _____

13. foil   _____

14. coin   _____

15. destroy   _____

Circle the correct spelling for each spelling word. Write the correct spelling on the line.

16. riplaise   replace   _____

17. wokked   walked   _____

18. sighedwok   sidewalk   _____

19. placed   plaised   _____

20. walking   wokking   _____

Compound Sentences

> **FOCUS** • A **compound sentence** is made when two sentences with related ideas are combined into one sentence. The sentences are connected with a conjunction.
>
> **Example:**
>
> Today I need to wash my clothes. Today I need to go to the grocery store.
>
> Today I need to wash my clothes, **and** I need to go to the grocery store.

PRACTICE Put an *X* next to the sentences that can be combined because they are about the same topic.

1. The dog barked. He wagged his tail. _____

2. Jason ran home. The sun was shining. _____

3. Seth hit the ball. He ran to first base. _____

4. The car was going fast. We were eating lunch. _____

5. Nick went to the phone. He answered it. _____

6. I like to watch old movies. My brother likes to listen to music. _____

7. Sean likes first grade. Harry went to preschool. _____

8. Nancy draws pictures of her friends. She gives them as gifts. _____

APPLY Complete the following sentences to make them compound sentences.

9. Josh took his dog for a walk, and _____

_____

10. The state of Georgia is above Florida, and _____

_____

11. Today I have two tests, but _____

_____

12. I do not know if I should take my dog, or _____

_____

13. I would like to take a lot of pictures during our vacation, but _____

_____

14. Lisa likes to talk on the phone, and _____

_____

15. My chore is to clean the living room, but _____

_____

16. Today I can eat pasta for dinner, or _____

_____

Fossils

Fossils give us clues about plants and animals that lived long ago. Scientists find most fossils buried in the ground. Have you ever seen a real fossil? Maybe you have seen a picture of a fossil. Have you ever seen a dinosaur bone? A dinosaur bone is a fossil!

There are different kinds of fossils. Some plants and animals died and were buried in mud. The mud got hard and turned into rock. Sometimes plants and animals left a print in the mud. Some of the prints were footprints. These prints turned into rocks too.

Scientists find fossils all over Earth. One of the main reasons to search for fossils is to learn more about what Earth was like long ago. Fossils provide a way to study plants and animals that are no longer alive on Earth.

Studying fossils is also a way to learn how old something is. Scientists have found fossils of the fern plant that is still alive today. That means ferns are very old!

Some of the most popular fossils are those of dinosaurs. Perhaps it is the mystery around dinosaurs that makes them so interesting. No living human has ever seen a living dinosaur. All we have are fossils.

There were lots of dinosaurs. The fossils that scientists find vary in size, but they all started off as bone. The dinosaur bones became fossils over time. Scientists collect these fossils and put them together to learn about the dinosaurs.

Sometimes the fossils are together in one place. They are the fossilized bones of the whole dinosaur. Other times the fossils are in different places. When that happens, the fossils are like pieces of a puzzle. Scientists examine each fossil. Then they put all of the fossils together for the correct dinosaur. They solve the puzzle.

So we know that fossils can come from plants as well as the bones of animals. Can you think of another kind of fossil? What about the whole body of an insect trapped inside a rock?

Some insects get stuck in the sticky liquid, or sap, that slides down the trunks of trees. Insects can get stuck in the sap. Over time, the sap gets hard. Once it becomes a solid it is called amber. Inside the amber is the body of the insect.

It is by studying the fossilized remains of animals and plants that we have any guesses about what they used to be like. Fossils are very helpful to both scientists and students. They help us learn about living things from the past.

Vocabulary

FOCUS Review the vocabulary words from "Election Day."

agreement	demonstrating	stocked
arranging	discipline	tolerant
ballots	errand	traditional
compassion	manager	training
courage	mock	

PRACTICE Write the vocabulary word that matches each synonym below.

1. sympathy _____

2. showing _____

3. bravery _____

4. focus _____

5. teaching _____

6. an understanding _____

7. organizing _____

8. filled _____

APPLY Write the vocabulary word that completes each pair of sentences below.

9. The woman ran the hardware store. The woman was a

   _____.

10. People put pieces of paper in the box in order to cast their votes. The people put _____ in the box.

11. The father took his two children with him when he went on a short trip to the store. The father ran an _____.

12. The Hungarian family sang a song that came out of the culture of their country. They sang a _____ song.

13. The boy tried to understand the customs of a pen pal who lived in another country. The boy tried to be

   _____.

14. The children pretended to be knights at a tournament. They held a _____ tournament.

15. The refrigerator was filled with all the food the family needed for the week. The refrigerator was _____.

Compare and Contrast

FOCUS
- To *compare* means to tell how things, events, or characters are alike. Some comparison clue words are *both, same, like,* and *too.*
- To *contrast* means to tell how things, events, or characters are different. Some contrast clue words are *different, but,* and *unlike.*

PRACTICE **Circle whether the sentence is comparing or contrasting. Then write the clue word on the line.**

1. The president and a Congresswoman are both people who work for the government.

   compare   **contrast**   _____

2. Unlike the United States, kings and queens rule some countries.

   compare   **contrast**   _____

3. A city and a town are both places people can choose to live.

   compare   **contrast**   _____

4. Men and woman both vote in United States' elections.

   compare   **contrast**   _____

APPLY Look again at "Election Day." Write two sentences comparing ways Erik and his mother acted as good citizens.

5. _____

6. _____

Write a sentence contrasting one of Erik's actions with actions of a student who did not behave like a good citizen.

7. _____

Write a sentence contrasting one of Erik's mother's actions with actions of an adult who was not behaving like a good citizen.

8. _____

The *ough* Spelling Pattern

> **FOCUS**
> - The *ough* spelling pattern has many different sounds.
> - The letter *t* at the end of the *ough* pattern will most often make the /aw/ sound.

PRACTICE Use the words in the box to answer the questions.

though	bought	dough	tough

1. Which words have the same vowel sound as *no*?

_____   _____

2. Which word has the same vowel sound as *saw*?

_____

3. Which word has the same vowel sound as *puff*?

_____

APPLY Add the given letter to the *ought spelling* pattern. Write the new word on the line.

4. s + ought = _____

5. f + ought = _____

6. b + ought = _____

7. br + ought = _____

Circle the correct word to complete each sentence.

8. Donna (bough, bought) apples at the market.

9. Do we have (enough, enought) chairs for everyone?

10. I (though, thought) class started at 8:30.

11. The children (fought, fough) over whose turn it was.

12. Use a rolling pin to flatten the cookie (dought, dough).

13. (Althought, Although) I live close to the school, I still ride the bus.

14. Raj (brought, bough) his tent for the camping trip.

15. We (sough, sought) sand and sun on our beach vacation.

Synonyms and Antonyms

FOCUS
- **Synonyms** are words that are similar in meaning. *Happy* and *glad* are synonyms.
- **Antonyms** are words that are opposite in meaning. *Up* and *down* are antonyms.

PRACTICE In each box, circle the *synonym* and draw a line under the *antonym* for each given word.

1. near	close	apart	far
2. winner	helper	loser	champion
3. before	beside	after	earlier

APPLY Write the *synonym* or *antonym* for the word in parentheses to complete the sentence.

4. (frown) Curtis has the warmest _____.

5. (bend) Slow down when you come to a _____ in the road.

6. (bright) Mom did not finish working until it was _____ outside, so we had a late dinner.

7. (hilarious) The _____ movie had us laughing all night long.

Multiple-Meaning Words and Homophones

> **FOCUS** **Multiple-meaning words** are spelled and pronounced the same but have different meanings.
> **Homophones** are words that are pronounced the same but have different spellings and meanings.

PRACTICE Use the multiple-meaning word and the homophones below to complete the sentences.

toad	towed	park

8. Can we _____ our car near the entrance to the _____?

9. Gina _____ the boat behind her truck.
   A _____ has bumpy skin, but a frog is smooth.

APPLY Read the two meanings for a multiple-meaning word. Write the word on the line.

10. the opposite of *left* **OR** correct _____

11. a person who swings at a ball **OR** a mixture used for making cake _____

Read the two meanings for a pair of homophones. Write the homophones on the lines.

12. belonging to us _____
    periods of time equal to 60 minutes _____

Name _____ **Date** _____

Vocabulary

> **FOCUS** Review the vocabulary words from "One Thousand and One Arabian Nights: Aladdin and the Wonderful Lamp."

acquainted	lord	spark
bazaar	meanwhile	spectacular
extraordinary	polished	sultan
fortune	procession	word

PRACTICE Synonyms mean the same or nearly the same thing. Match each vocabulary word with its synonym below.

1. procession   **a.** marketplace

2. bazaar   **b.** sultan

3. lord   **c.** familiar with

4. acquainted   **d.** march

5. spectacular   **e.** extraordinary

6. meanwhile   **f.** during

APPLY Read the definitions and the sentences.
Write the letter of the meaning that shows how the
underlined word is used in each sentence.

fortune a. chance or luck. **b.** a large amount of money.

7. _____ The sultan spent a <u>fortune</u> when he built
his palace.

word a. a meaningful element of speech, used with
others to make a sentence. **b.** a message or news.

8. _____ The messenger brought <u>word</u> of the new law.

spark a. a small, hot piece thrown from a fire.
b. a small piece of an intense feeling.

9. _____ A <u>spark</u> of anger began to burn in the
girl's heart.

polished a. shiny. **b.** elegant or fancy.

10. _____ The <u>polished</u> brass pot shone in the light.

Making Inferences

> **FOCUS** When you *make inferences,* you use information provided in a text, along with what you already know, to understand details the author did not put in the story.

PRACTICE Read each group of sentences.
Circle the correct *inference.*

1. Aladdin groaned and strained as he lifted the treasures. He could barely walk.
   a. The treasures were heavy.
   b. The treasures were expensive.

2. The boy rubbed his hands. He shivered.
   a. The boy was hot.
   b. The boy was cold.

3. The dog walked back and forth in front of the door. She whined. She walked over to her owner and nudged the owner's hand.
   a. The dog likes its food.
   b. The dog wants to go outside.

4. The mother put the treasure into a box. She locked it and hid the key.
   a. The mother wants more treasure.
   b. The mother wants to keep the treasure a secret.

APPLY Read each quote from "One Thousand and One Arabian Nights: Aladdin and the Wonderful Lamp." Use what you already know to answer each question that follows and make an inference.

"The sultan noticed the richness of the gifts. He saw that Aladdin himself was handsome and spoke well. This man was surely worthy of his daughter."

5. What inference can you make about what kind of husband the sultan wants for his daughter?

_____

_____

6. What information did you use to make this inference?

_____

_____

". . . she rubbed [the lamp] with a cloth. Immediately a genie appeared before them. "I am the genie of the lamp," the figure announced. 'What is your wish?'"

7. What inference can you make about the genie's rules for granting wishes?

_____

_____

8. What information did you use to make this inference?

_____

_____

Writing a Couplet

Think

Audience: *Who* will read your couplet?

_____

Purpose: *What* is your reason for writing a couplet?

_____

Prewriting

Use this graphic organizer to plan your couplet.

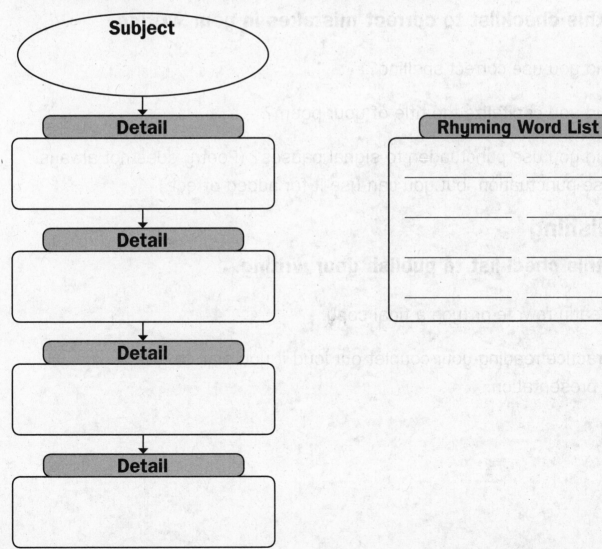

Subject

Detail

Detail

Detail

Detail

Rhyming Word List

Revising

Use this checklist to revise your writing.

☐ Does your poem meet your purpose for writing?

☐ Did you put rhyming words at the end of the lines?

☐ Did you use sensory adjectives?

☐ Did you use figurative language?

☐ Do your lines have the appropriate rhythm, or sound pattern?

☐ Does your poem create images that show feelings for the reader?

Editing/Proofreading

Use this checklist to correct mistakes in your writing.

☐ Did you use correct spelling?

☐ Did you capitalize the title of your poem?

☐ Did you use punctuation to signal pauses? (Poetry does not always use punctuation, but you can use it for added effect.)

Publishing

Use this checklist to publish your writing.

☐ Neatly rewrite or type a final copy.

☐ Practice reading your couplet out loud if you plan to give a presentation.

Name _____ **Date** _____

The *ough* Spelling Pattern; Compound Words; Homophones

FOCUS
- The spelling pattern *ough* can sound like /aw/, /ō/, /u/, and /o͞o/.
- Compound words are made up of two smaller words.
- Homophones are words that sound alike but have different meanings and spellings.

PRACTICE Sort the spelling words. Some words will appear under more than one heading.

ough with the /aw/ sound

1. _____

2. _____

ough with the /ō/ sound

3. _____

ough with the /u/ sound

4. _____

5. _____

ough with the /o͞o/ sound

6. _____

Two spelling words that are homophones

7. _____

8. _____

Word List		Challenge Words
1. cough	6. rough	11. thorough
2. dough	7. allowed	12. throughout
3. aloud	8. moonlight	13. thoughtful
4. through	9. pancake	14. foreword
5. thought	10. enough	15. forward

Two spelling words that are compound words

9. _____

10. _____

A homophone for *threw*

11. _____

One challenge word that is a compound word

12. _____

Two challenge words that are homophones

13. _____

14. _____

APPLY Circle the misspelled word in each sentence. Write the word correctly on the line.

15. I am not aloud to go to the park. _____

16. The train went threw the tunnel. _____

17. Please read allowed the book to me. _____

18. I kneaded the bread doe. _____

19. I moved my piece foreword in chess. _____

20. She did a through job on that project. _____

21. There is a forward in the front of the book. _____

22. I thawt of a great idea! _____

Review

FOCUS
- A **common noun** names a person, a place, a thing, or an idea.
- A **proper noun** names a *certain* person, place, or thing. A proper noun begins with a capital letter.
- An **action verb** tells what someone or something is doing.
- A **linking verb** connects the parts of a sentence to make it complete.
- A **helping verb** helps the main verb.
- The **subject** tells what or whom the sentence is about. The **predicate** tells what the subject is or does.

PRACTICE Write each noun under the correct column. Capitalize the proper nouns.

dancer	dr. green	color	brazil
snazzycola	book	tastyc's soup	class

Common Nouns

1. _____

2. _____

3. _____

4. _____

Proper Nouns

5. _____

6. _____

7. _____

8. _____

Read each sentence below. Circle the *subject*. Underline the *predicate*. On the line next to the sentence, write any words that need to start with capital letters.

9. the athletic girl threw the ball. _____

10. My best friend matt cheered loudly. _____

11. judy exercises every day. _____

12. My teacher read us flower power. _____

APPLY Read each sentence. Read the description of a noun or verb written in parentheses ( ). Write a *noun* or a *verb* on the line to complete the sentence.

13. _____ (proper noun) _____ (action verb) me how to play the piano.

14. My _____ (common noun) _____ (helping verb) swimming like a fish today.

15. That _____ (common noun) _____ (liking verb) my favorite.

Write three sentences using product names. Circle the *subject*, and underline the *predicate*. Be sure to begin each sentence with a capital letter.

16. _____

17. _____

18. _____

Silent Letters

FOCUS Silent letters in a word are not heard when the word is read.

PRACTICE Read each word. Circle the letter or letters that are silent.

1. hour
2. doubt
3. rhyming
4. scene
5. knit
6. wrench
7. lamb
8. island
9. scent
10. listen

11. crumb
12. school
13. adjust
14. knuckles
15. muscle
16. design
17. science
18. ache
19. thistle
20. autumn

APPLY Circle the correct word that completes each sentence.

21. Martin ate (hafe, **half**) of the sandwich.

22. Can you (**answer**, anser) the math question?

23. The (shent, **scent**) of roses filled the air.

24. Did you (**listen**, lissen) to the band play?

25. Cara hit her (thumn, **thumb**) with a hammer.

26. The (scine, **sign**) tells us which road to take.

Look at each pair of words with a silent-consonant spelling pattern. Underline the spelling pattern in each word. Write a third word with the same spelling pattern.

27. knee   knot   _____

28. climb   numb   _____

29. wrong   wrist   _____

30. gnat   sign   _____

31. rhombus   rhythm   _____

32. taught   daughter   _____

The Prefixes *dis-*, *un-*, and *non-*

FOCUS A **prefix** is added to the beginning of a word and changes the meaning of that word.
- The prefix **dis-** means "to do the opposite of" or "not to."
- The prefix **un-** means "the opposite of" or "not."
- The prefix **non-** means "to do the opposite of" or "not."

PRACTICE Choose a prefix from above to add to each base word. Write the meaning of the new word.

1. _____stop _____

2. _____agree _____

3. _____planned _____

4. _____loyal _____

5. _____wind _____

6. _____fiction _____

7. _____zip _____

8. _____connect _____

APPLY Choose one of the following prefixes to add to the base word in parentheses ( ) to form a new word that completes the sentence. Write the new word on the line. Then write the meaning of the new word.

dis-	un-	non-

9. Karl was (able) _____ to attend the party.

New Meaning: _____

10. You must speak to the principal if you (obey) _____ your teacher.

New Meaning: _____

11. Joan (wrapped) _____ her birthday gift.

New Meaning: _____

12. We use (toxic) _____ cleaners that are safe for the environment.

New Meaning: _____

13. Please (connect) _____ your phone from the charger.

New Meaning: _____

14. Toby uses (fat) _____ milk on his cereal.

New Meaning: _____

Word Analysis • *Skills Practice 2*

Vocabulary

> **FOCUS** Review the vocabulary words from "The Art of Storytelling."

account	**generation**	**stir**
civilizations	**impression**	**styles**
fond	**organizations**	**tablets**
founded	**spark**	**wonder**

PRACTICE Match each word with its definition below.

1. stir   **a.** one step in line from an ancestor

2. fond   **b.** loving

3. impression   **c.** an effect on the mind

4. founded   **d.** to excite

5. civilizations   **e.** highly-developed human societies

6. generation   **f.** started

APPLY Circle the vocabulary word or words that complete each pair of sentences below.

7. Cuneiform was an ancient system of writing. Sumerians first developed it 5,000 years ago as a way to keep (civilizations, accounts) of history.

8. Other people living nearby learned about cuneiform. This way of writing made a big (tablet, impression) on them.

9. The invention of cuneiform (sparked, account) the beginning of written records. It was a new way to keep track of stories and information.

10. To make cuneiform, people used a special stick, called a stylus. They pressed the stylus into clay (tablets, generations).

11. Cuneiform was used for many (generations, styles). Over time, people developed different (wonder, styles) of cuneiform.

12. At first, one drawing stood for something you could touch or see with your eyes, like a king. Later, the drawings came to mean ideas or feelings such as (wonder, tablets) or sorrow.

Name _____ **Date** _____

Classify and Categorize

> **FOCUS** Classifying and categorizing help you organize information. It is a way of putting people, animals, and objects into different groups. It can help you see ways things are alike and different. It can also help you remember important ideas.

PRACTICE Read each group of items below. Write a category title for a group all the items could belong in.

1. paintbrush, paper, art books
   What category could these all belong in? _____

2. shoes, boots, sandals
   What category could these all belong in? _____

3. plays, movies, television
   What category could these all belong in? _____

4. cars, trucks, trains
   What category could these all belong in? _____

APPLY In "The Art of Storytelling," the author describes different types of storytelling. Name two ways people tell each other stories. Explain your reasons for classifying them this way.

5. _____ belongs in this category

because _____.

6. _____ belongs in this category

because _____.

Find the heading "Early Storytelling through Images." Use information the author classified under this heading to help you name two types of early storytelling.

7. _____

8. _____

Use information from the chapter "Storytelling through Sound and Movement" to classify examples of sound and movement storytelling.

9. One type of sound storytelling: _____

10. One type of movement storytelling: _____

Responding to Literature

Think

Audience: *Who* will read your response to literature?

_____

Purpose: *What* is your reason for writing a response
to literature?

_____

Prewriting

Use the story map below to plan your response to
literature. Fill in the main events from the beginning,
middle, and ending of the story.

Plot

Beginning (problem)	Middle (events)	Ending (how problem is solved)

Revising

Use this checklist to revise your writing.

- [ ] Does your response include the most important events from the story?

- [ ] Did you use temporal words to describe the sequence of events?

- [ ] Did you use terms such as *beginning, middle, end,* and *plot*?

- [ ] Did you add details from the story that were left out of your draft?

- [ ] Do you use formal language?

Editing/Proofreading

Use this checklist to correct mistakes in your writing.

- [ ] Did you use correct spelling?

- [ ] Does every sentence and proper noun begin with a capital letter?

- [ ] Does every sentence end with the correct punctuation mark?

- [ ] Did you use compound sentences?

Publishing

Use this checklist to publish your writing.

- [ ] Neatly rewrite or type a final copy of your response to literature.

- [ ] Include an illustration of one of the events from the story.

Silent Letters; Prefixes *dis-*, *un-*, and *non-*

FOCUS
- Silent letters are letters in a word that are not heard when the word is pronounced.
- The prefix *dis-* means "the opposite of" or "not."
- The prefix *un-* means "the opposite of" or "not."
- The prefix *non-* means "not."

PRACTICE **Sort the spelling words.**

Silent *t*

1. _____

2. _____

Silent *h*

3. _____

Silent *w*

4. _____

Silent *l*

5. _____

Prefix *dis-*

6. _____

Prefix *un-*

7. _____

8. _____

Prefix *non-*

9. _____

10. _____

Word List		Challenge Words
1. listen	**6.** unscrew	**11.** discover
2. castle	**7.** unharmed	**12.** scenic
3. answer	**8.** nondairy	**13.** rhyme
4. nonslip	**9.** could	**14.** unfriendly
5. rhino	**10.** distract	**15.** rhythm

APPLY

Read each word below. If the word is spelled correctly, write *correct* on the line. If the word is misspelled, write the correctly spelled word on the line.

11. ancer _____

12. distract _____

13. could _____

14. rino _____

15. unsceroo _____

16. nonslip _____

17. casul _____

18. listen _____

19. nondarry _____

20. unharmed _____

Review

> **FOCUS**
> - A **complete sentence** has a subject and a predicate. In an incomplete sentence, the subject or predicate is missing.
> - A **declarative** sentence makes a statement and ends in a **period** (.). An **interrogative** sentence asks a question and ends in a **question mark** (?). An **imperative** sentence gives direction and ends in a **period** (.). An **exclamatory** sentence shows strong feeling and ends in an **exclamation point** (!).
> - The first letter of the first word in a sentence is **capitalized**.

PRACTICE In the sentences below, triple-underline the letters that should be capitalized. Add correct end marks. On the line, identify the type of sentence by writing *D* (declarative), *IN* (interrogative), *IM* (imperative), or *E* (exclamatory).

1. my grandfather came to this country from ireland many years ago _____

2. his name was dr. allen gardener _____

3. have you researched any of your ancestors _____

4. go to the library to learn how to do the research _____

5. it's really exciting _____

6. leave immediately _____

APPLY In the paragraph below, triple-underline the letters that should be capitalized, and add correct end marks.

do you know where your ancestors came from Your ancestors are the members of your family who lived before you most people have ancestors who came to America from another country Is your family from one country or many countries freedom, money, and safety are some of the reasons people come to this country would you be afraid to move to a distant country our ancestors were very brave people I love learning about my ancestors

Add missing subjects or predicates to the sentences below and rewrite them as complete sentences.

7. Under the picnic table.

_____

8. The squirrels in the tree.

_____

9. After my brother came home.

_____

10. The swimming pool at the park.

_____

The *ough* Spelling Pattern

FOCUS
- The *ough* spelling pattern has many different sounds.
- Adding the letter *t* to the end of the *ough* pattern makes the /aw/ sound.

PRACTICE Sort the words under the correct heading.

rough	though	ought

/aw/ vowel sound

1. _____

/u/ vowel sound

3. _____

/ō/ vowel sound

2. _____

APPLY Circle the correct word that completes each sentence.

4. Brad (thought, though) the party was a success.

5. Jamal was (therow, thorough) when he cleaned his room.

6. (Althought, Although) Tara is young, she is very wise.

7. The bitter medicine is (tough, though) to swallow.

8. We (fawt, fought) the rapids as we paddled along the river.

Silent Letters

PRACTICE Choose a letter in parentheses ( ) to complete each word. Write the letter on the line.

9. (g, h) desi_____n

10. (m, n) colum_____

11. (h, k) sc_____ool

12. (s, t) cas_____le

13. (c, h) s_____issors

14. (b, n) num_____

15. (g, k) _____nock

APPLY Unscramble the following words, and then write each new word on the line. Underline the silent letter or letters in each word.

16. t c n e s _____

17. o b t u d _____

18. l e w e s r t _____

19. w e n k _____

20. u s m l e c _____

21. m u t a n u _____

22. d h c r o _____

The Prefixes *re-*, *pre-*, and *mis-*

FOCUS A **prefix** is added to the beginning of a word and changes the meaning of that word.

- The prefix *re-* means "again" or "back."

- The prefix *pre-* means "before in place, time, or order."

- The prefix *mis-* means "bad," "wrong," or "incorrectly."

PRACTICE Add a prefix to each base word. Write the new word. Then write the meaning of the new word.

1. mis + judge = _____

New Meaning: _____

2. re + play = _____

New Meaning: _____

3. mis + spell = _____

New Meaning: _____

4. pre + cook = _____

New Meaning: _____

5. re + mix = _____

New Meaning: _____

6. pre + select = _____

New Meaning: _____

APPLY Choose one of the following prefixes to add to the base word in parentheses ( ) to form a new word that completes the sentence. Write the new word on the line. Then write the meaning of the new word.

re-	pre-	mis-

7. If you (treat) _____ a car, it won't run properly.

New Meaning: _____

8. Press the backward arrow to (wind) _____ the song.

New Meaning: _____

9. Libby (cut) _____ some fabric before starting the quilt.

New Meaning: _____

10. The piano needs to be (tuned) _____ after we move to the new house.

New Meaning: _____

11. We (ordered) _____ tickets months before the show.

New Meaning: _____

12. Chris (places) _____ his phone every day, but he always finds it!

New Meaning: _____

Vocabulary

> **FOCUS** Review the vocabulary words from "Cinderlad."

abruptly	clearing	eligible	scaled
amused	desire	moaned	strolled

PRACTICE Decide whether the definition after each sentence gives the correct meaning of the underlined word in the sentence. Circle *Correct* or *Incorrect*.

1. The prince <u>scaled</u> the walls of the castle.

Definition: "climbed over the top of"

Correct   **Incorrect**

2. The deer came into an open <u>clearing</u> in the woods.

Definition: "an area with many trees"

Correct   **Incorrect**

3. The <u>amused</u> sisters laughed at the joke.

Definition: "feeling enjoyment"

Correct   **Incorrect**

4. The man <u>strolled</u> slowly along the path.

Definition: "ran quickly"

Correct   **Incorrect**

APPLY Circle vocabulary words to complete the story below.

Some Native people of Canada tell their own Cinderella story. In this story, Mighty Wind was the name of a brave hunter. Mighty Wind had many skills. He could **5.** (scale, moan) the sides of high mountains. He could run very fast.

What was most impressive about Mighty Wind, however, was that, without warning, he could **6.** (abruptly, amused) become invisible. Then, only Mighty Wind's sister could see him.

The chief of Mighty Wind's village had three daughters. These women were all **7.** (eligible, strolled) to be married soon. The older two were cruel to the youngest sister. Even when she **8.** (strolled, moaned) or cried, they did not treat her kindly.

The two older sisters **9.** (amused, desired) to marry brave Mighty Wind. He decided to put them to the test. His sister asked if they could see him as he walked along the beach. "Oh, yes," they each lied. When she asked them to describe the ropes he used to pull his sled, they could not.

Then the youngest sister went to where Mighty Wind **10.** (strolled, scaled) beside the water. The youngest sister was honest, and admitted, "I cannot see him." Mighty Wind chose to marry the youngest sister because she was truthful.

Sequence

FOCUS
- *Sequence* is the order in which events in a story occur. Writers often use time-and-order words to help readers understand the sequence of events.
- *Time* words (*winter, 1900, minutes*) show the passage of time.
- *Order* words (*first, next, later*) show the order in which events happen.

PRACTICE **Read this paragraph carefully. Write the *time* and *order* words on the lines below.**

Between the 1100s and 1500s, Europe had a special kind of entertainer called a minstrel. In the early days, most minstrels wandered and played for lords and ladies. Later, the minstrels organized groups called guilds. Finally, by the 1600s, the job of the minstrel was no longer as important.

Time words

1. _____

2. _____

3. _____

4. _____

Order words

5. _____

6. _____

APPLY Think about "Cinderlad." Use what you know from the text to answer the sequence questions below.

7. Write the order in which the brothers protect the meadow. Use the words *first, next,* and *finally*.

_____

_____

_____

8. Does this order matter? Give reasons to support your answer.

_____

_____

9. Write the order in which Cinderlad wears the different suits of armor. Use the words *first, next,* and *finally*.

_____

_____

_____

10. Does this order matter? Give reasons to support your answer.

_____

_____

Persuasive Writing

Think

Audience: *Who* will read your persuasive writing?

_____

_____

Purpose: *What* is your reason for writing to persuade?

_____

_____

Prewriting

Choose reasons for your opinion that will persuade others to agree with you. Then choose the three best reasons.

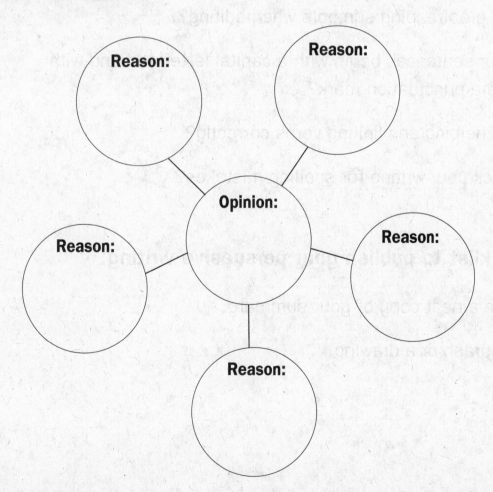

Revising

Use this checklist to revise your persuasive writing.

☐ Does your writing state an opinion?

☐ Does your writing have reasons that will appeal to your audience?

☐ Does your writing use precise words to describe the topic and reasons?

☐ Is your writing's purpose clearly to persuade?

☐ Did you use language that is appropriate for your audience?

Editing/Proofreading

Use this checklist to correct mistakes in your persuasive writing.

☐ Did you use proofreading symbols when editing?

☐ Do all of your sentences begin with a capital letter and end with an appropriate punctuation mark?

☐ Did you use helping and linking verbs correctly?

☐ Did you check your writing for spelling mistakes?

Publishing

Use this checklist to publish your persuasive writing.

☐ Write or type a neat copy of your summary.

☐ Add a photograph or a drawing.

The *ough* Spelling Pattern; Silent Letters; Prefixes *re-*, *pre-*, and *mis-*

FOCUS
- The spelling pattern *ough* can sound like /aw/, /ō/, /u/, and /o͞o/.
- Silent letters are letters in a word that are not heard when the word is pronounced.
- The prefix *re-* means "again" or "back."
- The prefix *pre-* means "before."
- The prefix *mis-* means "bad," "wrong," or "incorrectly."

PRACTICE Sort the spelling words.

ough with the /aw/ sound

1. _____

2. _____

ough with the /ō/ sound

3. _____

Silent letter t

4. _____

Silent letter k

5. _____

Silent letter b

6. _____

Prefix re-

7. _____

Prefix pre-

8. _____

9. _____

Prefix mis-

10. _____

Word List		Challenge Words
1. whistle	**6.** debt	**11.** exhaust
2. fought	**7.** misjudge	**12.** reappear
3. preorder	**8.** predawn	**13.** rearrange
4. trough	**9.** although	**14.** preseason
5. replace	**10.** knew	**15.** mispronounce

APPLY Read each word below. If the word is spelled correctly, write *correct* on the line. If the word is misspelled, write the correctly spelled word on the line.

11. fot _____

12. misjudge _____

13. wislle _____

14. riplase _____

15. troff _____

16. preorder _____

17. nue _____

18. predonn _____

19. although _____

20. debt _____

Review

> ***FOCUS***
> - An **adjective** is a word that describes a noun.
>   It tells *how much*, *how many*, or *what kind*.
>   A **comparative adjective** compares nouns
>   or pronouns.
> - An **article** is a special kind of adjective.
>   The three articles are *a, an,* and *the.*
> - A **singular noun** names one of something.
>   A **plural noun** names more than one.
> - A **quotation mark** is used right before and right
>   after the words a speaker says.
> - A **comma** is used to separate a quotation from
>   the person who said it.
> - **Capitalize** the days of the week, the months,
>   the names of holidays, and the names of
>   cities, states, and other geographic places.

PRACTICE **In the paragraph below, triple-underline
letters that should be capitalized. Single-underline
comparative adjectives, and circle plural nouns.**

Did you know china has the world's largest
population? India is the next biggest, then the united
states, and then indonesia. The three states with the
largest population in the U.S. are california, texas,
and new york. The largest state in the mainland united
states is texas, and california is bigger than new york.
Of the cities in these states, New York City has the
biggest population. The next biggest city is los angeles,
which is in california.

APPLY In the paragraph below, underline the articles. Circle the adjectives and comparative adjectives, and triple-underline any letters that should be capitalized.

In october my family traveled to china to see where our ancestors came from. We left the united states on labor day, which was a monday. We arrived in China on wednesday. The bumpy airplane ride felt like the longest three days of my life. We had packed enough shirts, shorts, and shoes to last for five weeks. My suitcase was heavy, but my sister's was heavier. She had a hard time carrying it through the airport. We stayed in China until november. What a great trip!

List the plural form of the nouns below.

lunch   tooth   dress   deer   mouse   radius

_____   _____   _____

_____   _____   _____

Rewrite each sentence below, so it uses quotation marks and commas correctly.

1. Tell me about your day said Aunt Larissa.

_____

_____

2. Dr. Stone said Your heart sounds healthy and strong."

_____

_____

Contrast /o͞o/ with /oo/ and /ō/ with /ow/

> **FOCUS**
> - The *oo* spelling pattern can make the /o͞o/ and /oo/ sounds.
> - The *u, u_e, _ue,* and *_ew* spelling patterns can make the /o͞o/ sound.
> - The *ow* spelling pattern can make the /ō/ sound or the /ow/ sound.

PRACTICE Write the following words under the correct sound.

crowded	yellow	rookie	booth
owner	drowsy	groomer	childhood

/o͞o/

1. _____

2. _____

/oo/

3. _____

4. _____

/ō/

5. _____

6. _____

/ow/

7. _____

8. _____

APPLY Unscramble the letters in parentheses ( ) to
make a word with the given spelling pattern.

9. (r, c) _____ow

10. (g, d, l) _____ue_____

11. (h, s, p) _____oo_____

12. (r, f, e, l) _____ow_____

13. (l, s, a, h, l) _____ow

14. (t, t, h, r) _____u_____

Write a word for each spelling pattern listed below.

15. /ō/ spelled *ow* _____

16. /ow/ spelled *ow* _____

17. /oo/ spelled *oo* _____

18. /o͞o/ spelled *oo* _____

19. /o͞o/ spelled *u* _____

20. /o͞o/ spelled _*ue* _____

21. /o͞o/ spelled *u_e* _____

22. /o͞o/ spelled _*ew* _____

Comparatives and Superlatives

> **FOCUS**
> - The **comparative ending** -er shows a comparison between two things.
> - The **superlative ending** -est shows a comparison among three or more things.
> - Some words that show comparisons do not follow the usual patterns of adding -er or -est. These words are **irregular comparatives**.

PRACTICE Add -er or -est to the following words. Write each new word on the line.

1. fresh + er = _____

2. safe + est = _____

3. angry + est = _____

4. loud + er = _____

5. wet + er = _____

6. narrow + est = _____

APPLY Choose a word from the box to complete each sentence.

most	better	farther	least	worse	farthest

7. Jake hopes he sleeps _____ tonight than he did last night.

8. Five students made paper airplanes, and Rosie's flew the _____.

9. The winner is the person who scores the _____ points.

10. Buddy is a good dog and causes the _____ trouble of any pet I know.

11. The doctor said to call if my pain gets _____.

12. Is it _____ to walk to the school or the store?

Suffixes *-er*, *-or*, and *-ness*

> **FOCUS**
> - A **suffix** is added to the end of a base word. Adding a suffix changes the meaning of the word.
> - The suffixes **-er** and **-or** can mean "one who." It refers to a person or thing that does a certain action. **Examples:** eraser (a thing that erases) actor (one who acts)
> - The suffix **-ness** means "the state of being." **Example:** shyness (the state of being shy)

PRACTICE Add the suffix *-er*, *-or*, or *-ness* to the base words below. Write the new word, and then write its meaning.

13. toast + er = _____

14. sail + or = _____

15. calm + ness = _____

APPLY Add the suffix *-er*, *-or*, or *-ness* to a word from the box. Then write the word to complete a sentence.

fond	senate	sweep	bumpy	jog

16. A _____ is elected by the people in his or her state.

17. Marley's vivid outfits show her _____ of bright colors.

18. The _____ of the road caused me to feel sick.

19. Use a _____ to clean the floor.

20. We passed a _____ on the path in the park.

Vocabulary

> **Focus** Review the vocabulary words from "Cinderella Tales."

compelled	rivaled
dismayed	summoned
grace	transformed
opportunity	unfortunately

PRACTICE Antonyms are words that mean the opposite of each other. Read each group of words below. Write the vocabulary word that is an antonym.

1. pleased, gladdened, overjoyed

Antonym: _____

2. luckily, happily, fortunately

Antonym: _____

3. stopped, hindered, discouraged

Antonym: _____

4. rudeness, clumsiness, crudeness

Antonym: _____

APPLY Write a vocabulary word to complete each sentence below.

5. Characters in fairy tales have the _____ to make choices no one can in real life.

6. For example, Aladdin _____ a genie by rubbing a lamp and a ring, and then had to decide what to wish.

7. In the fairy tale "Snow White," Snow White's amazing beauty _____ that of the mean queen's, and the queen discovered this by use of a special talking mirror.

8. In many tales bad people are _____ into animals because of their evil deeds.

9. In some stories, like "Beauty and the Beast," such a character learns _____ and kindness and then is able to transform back into a person.

10. Even though these stories are not realistic, their morals and lessons _____ listeners to choose good over evil.

Compare and Contrast

> **FOCUS**
> - To *compare* means to tell how things, events, or characters are alike. Some comparison clue words are *both*, *same*, *like*, and *too*.
> - To *contrast* means to tell how things, events, or characters are different. Some contrast clue words are *while*, *but*, and *unlike*.

PRACTICE Circle whether the sentence is comparing or contrasting. Then write the clue word on the line.

1. The sun is a star, while Earth is a planet.

compare   **contrast**   _____

2. Like people in France, people in China have told their own "Cinderella" stories.

compare   **contrast**   _____

3. Both Noh and Kabuki are types of Japanese dance theatre.

compare   **contrast**   _____

4. Books used to be very expensive, but now they are very cheap.

compare   **contrast**   _____

APPLY Look again at "Cinderella Tales."
Write two sentences comparing the different
"Cinderella" characters in the stories.

5. _____

_____

_____

6. _____

_____

_____

Write one sentence contrasting the men
the "Cinderella" characters marry.

7. _____

_____

_____

Compare or contrast one of the characters in
"Cinderella Tales" with one of the characters
from "Cinderlad."

8. _____

_____

_____

Access Complex Text • *Skills Practice 2*

Thank-You Note

Think

Audience: *Who* will read your thank-you note?

_____

Purpose: *What* is your reason for writing a
thank-you note?

_____

Prewriting

Use this graphic organizer to plan your thank-you note.

Date _____ Return Address

Greeting _____

Body

_____

_____

_____

_____

Closing _____

Signature _____

Address for Envelope

Revising

Use this checklist to revise your writing.

☐ Is the reason for writing your thank-you note clear?

☐ Did you include all the parts of a note?

☐ Are the sentences in a clear order?

☐ Did you use formal language?

☐ Does your thank-you note sound friendly and polite?

Editing/Proofreading

Use this checklist to correct mistakes in your writing.

☐ Did you use commas and capitalization correctly in the greeting and closing?

☐ Does every name begin with a capital letter?

☐ Is every word or special term spelled correctly?

☐ Does each sentence begin with a capital letter and end with the correct punctuation mark?

Publishing

Use this checklist to publish your writing.

☐ Write or type a neat copy of your writing.

☐ Address an envelope to mail your letter.

Contrast /o͞o/ and /oo/; Contrast /ō/ and /ow/; Comparatives and Superlatives; Suffixes -er, -or, and -ness

FOCUS
- The *oo* spelling makes different sounds /oo/ and /o͞o/ like *cook* and *room*.
- The *ow* spelling can make the sound /ō/, and the /ow/ like *low* and *cow*.
- The **comparative ending** -er shows a comparison between two things. The **superlative ending** -est between three or more things.
- The suffixes -er and -or mean "one who."
- The suffix -ness means "the state of being."

PRACTICE Sort the spelling words.

ow as in *flow*

1. _____

ow as in *now*

2. _____

/oo/ sound

3. _____

/o͞o/ sound

4. _____

Comparative ending -er

5. _____

Superlative ending -est

6. _____

Word List
1. tighter
2. boot
3. took
4. somehow
5. arrow
6. deepest
7. worse
8. speaker
9. visitor
10. weakness

Challenge Words
11. driftwood
12. typhoon
13. director
14. downtown
15. borrow

Irregular comparative

7. _____

Suffix -or

9. _____

Suffix -er

8. _____

Suffix -ness

10. _____

APPLY **Write the spelling word that rhymes with each pair of words below.**

11. shoot   root   _____

12. shook   hook   _____

13. bellow   meadow   _____

14. plow   how   _____

Circle the correctly spelled word. Then write the correctly spelled word on the line.

15. deepest   depist   _____

16. weeknis   weakness   _____

17. speeker   speaker   _____

18. tighter   titer   _____

19. worse   wirse   _____

20. visiter   visitor   _____

Review

> **FOCUS**
> - A **comma** is used after each item in a series or list of things, except after the last one.
> - A **colon** is used to introduce a list or to separate the hour from the minutes when writing time.
> - A sentence must have **subject and verb agreement.** This means the subject and the verb must both be singular, or they must both be plural.
> - An **adverb** is a word that describes a verb by telling *how*, *where*, or *when*.
> - A **collective noun** describes a group of people or things. Collective nouns are singular nouns.

PRACTICE For the paragraph below, put *colons* and *commas* in the correct places. Underline the *adverbs*.

My family arrived safely at the powwow at 2 30. It was an interesting event. There were dancers storytellers and people selling crafts. I saw people making the following items blankets baskets and moccasins. My brother's favorite part was the fry bread. He quickly ate once piece and then bought a second one. When we go next year, I will definitely bring a camera.

APPLY Circle the verb that correctly completes each sentence by agreeing with the subject in number.

1. We (are, is) going to the park after school.

2. A squirrel (are, is) a type of mammal.

3. They (has, have) been enjoying the music.

4. The herd of deer (head, heads) into the forest.

5. The rainforest (has, have) many plants and animals.

6. Max (fix, fixes) the handlebars of his bike.

Write two sentence that use adverbs.

7. _____

   _____

8. _____

   _____

Circle the correct word. Then identify its part of speech.

9. The (quiet, quietly) girl studied hard. _____

10. He worked (busy, busily) around the house. _____

11. She worked very (hard, hardly) on the project. _____

12. The (fast, fastly) boy rode his bike home. _____

Grammar • *Skills Practice 2*

Contrast /o͞o/ with /ū/ and /aw/ with /ow/

FOCUS
- The /o͞o/ and /ū/ sounds can be spelled *u, u_e, _ue,* and *_ew.*
- The /aw/ sound can be spelled *aw* and *au_.*
- The /ow/ sound can be spelled *ow* and *ou_.*

PRACTICE Underline the /ow/ or /aw/ spelling pattern in each word. Write a rhyming word that has the same spelling pattern.

1. crown _____

2. pause _____

3. sound _____

4. claw _____

5. shower _____

6. yawn _____

Read the clue and fill in the correct /o͞o/ or /ū/ spelling pattern to complete the word.

7. a person   h _____ man

8. to say no   ref _____ s _____

9. a thick soup   st _____

10. a spring flower   t _____ lip

11. to disagree   arg _____

12. to make dirty   poll _____ t _____

APPLY **Circle the correct word that completes each sentence.**

13. What interesting shapes do you see in the _____?

    a. clowds   **b.** clouds   **c.** clauds   **d.** cloweds

14. Does the cost of a meal _____ a drink?

    a. inclewd   **b.** includ   **c.** inclued   **d.** include

15. Grandma's ring has great _____ to Jenny.

    a. value   **b.** valew   **c.** valu   **d.** valaue

16. A kite was _____ in the tree's branches.

    a. cought   **b.** cawght   **c.** caut   **d.** caught

17. You can count on Manny to always tell the _____.

    a. trueth   **b.** truth   **c.** truthe   **d.** trouth

18. The _____ of the storm caused a lot of damage.

    a. furye   **b.** furry   **c.** fury   **d.** furey

19. We heard wolves _____ in the distance.

    a. houl   **b.** howl   **c.** hawl   **d.** howel

20. I need to _____ this library book.

    a. renu   **b.** reknew   **c.** renue   **d.** renew

Suffixes *-ly*, *-y*, *-able*, *-ment* and Word Families

FOCUS • A **suffix** is added to the end of a base word and changes the meaning of the word.

The suffix *-ly* means "in a certain way."

The suffix *-y* means "like" or "full of."

The suffix *-able* means "able to be or worthy of being" or "tending toward."

The suffix *-ment* means "the act, process, or result of" or "the condition of being."

• A **base word** is a word that can stand alone. A base word can give a clue to the meaning of other words in the **word family.**

Example: base word—kind
word family—unkind, kindly, kindness, kindest

PRACTICE Add the suffix *-ly*, *-y*, *-able*, or *-ment* to the base words below. Write the new word and the meaning of the new word.

Base Word	Suffix	New Word	New Meaning
1. sincere +	ly =	_____	_____
2. ship +	ment =	_____	_____
3. chew +	able =	_____	_____
4. ice +	y =	_____	_____

Write the base word for each word family below.

5. likely, unlike, likable

base word: _____

6. unworthy, worthwhile, worthless

base word: _____

7. investor, reinvest, investment

base word: _____

APPLY Circle the words in the same word family.
Then write the base word on the line.

8. shaky   shacks   shakable

base word: _____

9. easy   easily   eastern

base word: _____

10. convertible   comforter   converter

base word: _____

11. devalue   developer   development

base word: _____

12. screamer   creamy   creamer

base word: _____

13. correctly   contractor   incorrect

base word: _____

14. manager   management   angrily

base word: _____

Vocabulary

> ***Focus*** Review the vocabulary words from "Storytelling:
> A Zulu Tradition."

carving	deeds	oral
certain	exist	praise
clever	likewise	riddles
contains	member	stain

PRACTICE Match each word or phrase with its example below.

1. oral folktale

2. a carving

3. characters that do not exist in real life

4. something the ocean contains

5. a riddle

a. What is black and white and red all over?

b. a piece of art cut from wood

c. "How Stories Came to Be"

d. water

e. King and Queen of the Water People

APPLY *Synonyms* are words that mean the same or nearly the same thing. Write the vocabulary word that is a synonym for each underlined word or words below.

King of the Birds: A Zulu Folktale

All the birds argued about who should be king. A <u>particular</u> **6.** _____ tiny bird, called a warbler, piped up and he should be king. The bigger birds laughed, but then they all agreed that their <u>actions</u> **7.** _____ would show who deserved to be king.

They decided to see which <u>associate</u> **8.** _____ of the bird group could fly highest. They all began to fly. <u>Smart</u> **9.** _____ warbler hid under eagle's wing. When eagle flew high, warbler darted out and flew the highest of all.

Rather than <u>speak well of</u> **10.** _____ warbler, the other birds were angry. They wanted to catch and punish warbler.

Owl watched for warbler for a long time, but he fell asleep and warbler escaped. With this <u>mark</u> **11.** _____ on his reputation, owl now hides all day, and only hunts at night.

Warbler, <u>also</u>, **12.** _____ no longer flies freely, but flits from branch to branch. He does not want the other birds to catch him.

Main Idea and Details

FOCUS
- The *main idea* tells what a paragraph is about. It is the most important idea presented by the author.
- *Details* provide specific information about the *main idea*.

PRACTICE Circle the detail that does NOT belong with each underlined main idea below.

1. <u>Oral storytelling has been a way for cultures to teach people lessons.</u> People have told stories to teach people about good actions. Some stories demonstrated what happens to evildoers. Cultures have many art forms.

2. <u>Water can exist in three forms.</u> Water is a good drink. Liquid water takes the shape of its container. Frozen water is a solid. Water vapor is a gas.

3. <u>Hiking is a fun hobby.</u> People who hike get to experience nature firsthand. Hikers get good exercise. Model trains are another hobby.

4. <u>There are many people groups in Africa.</u> The Zulu people live in southern Africa. Africa is one of the seven continents. The Sukuma people live in eastern Africa.

APPLY Think about what you learned from "Storytelling: A Zulu Tradition." Look at each group of details below. Write a main idea that could go with the details to form a paragraph.

5. Main Idea: _____

Details: People tell stories to share their history. People use stories to teach lessons about life. Stories can praise people's good actions.

6. Main Idea: _____

Details: Zulu people made clothing and beaded jewelry. They created pots out of clay. They wove baskets and mats.

Think about what you learned about stories in "The Art of Storytelling" and "Storytelling: A Zulu Tradition." Look at the main idea below. Use information from both selections to write two details to go with it.

Main Idea: Books are not the only way people tell stories.

7. _____

_____

8. _____

_____

Personal Narrative

Think

Audience: *Who* will read your personal narrative?

_____

Purpose: *What* is your reason for writing a personal narrative?

_____

Prewriting

Use the web below to think of sensory details you can include in your personal narrative. Write the event you are describing in the center box. Then write sensory details in the outer boxes. Try to think of a detail for at least four of the five senses: sight, hearing, smell, taste, and touch.

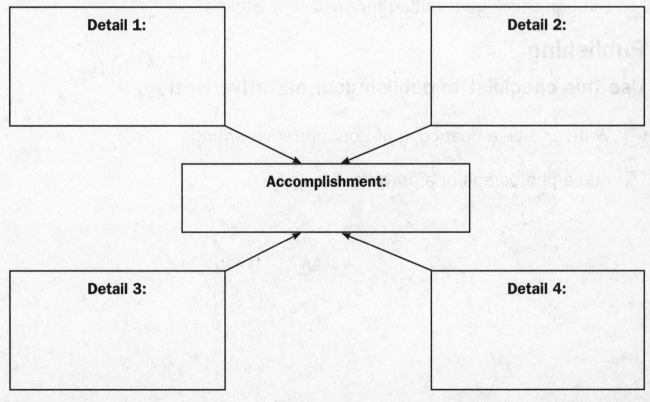

Detail 1:

Detail 2:

Accomplishment:

Detail 3:

Detail 4:

Revising

Use this checklist to revise your narrative writing.

☐ Does your writing describe your accomplishment?

☐ Did you include descriptive details?

☐ Does your story have a beginning, middle, and ending?

☐ Did you use a consistent point of view?

Editing/Proofreading

Use this checklist to correct mistakes in your narrative writing.

☐ Did you use proofreading symbols when editing?

☐ Do all of your sentences begin with a capital letter and end with an appropriate punctuation mark?

☐ Did you use verb tenses correctly?

☐ Did you check your writing for spelling mistakes?

Publishing

Use this checklist to publish your narrative writing.

☐ Write or type a neat copy of your narrative writing.

☐ Add a photograph or a drawing.

Contrast /o͞o/ with /ū/; Contrast /aw/ with /ow/; Suffixes *-ly*, *-y*, *-able*, and *-ment*; Words with the Same Base

FOCUS
- The *u* spelling makes different sounds. One sound is /ū/, as in *fuse*. Another sound is /o͞o/, as in *rule*.
- The /aw/ sound can be spelled *aw*, as in the word *lawn*. The /ow/ sound can be spelled *ow*, as in the word *gown*.
- The suffix *-ly* means "in a certain way,"*-y* means "full of," *-able* means "capable of and suited for," *-ment* means "the action or process of doing something."
- A group of words may share the same base word.

PRACTICE Sort the spelling words. Two words will fit under more than one heading.

/o͞o/ sound

1. _____

/ū/ sound

2. _____

/aw/ sound

3. _____

Word List		Challenge Words
1. flower	**6.** secure	**11.** computer
2. flaw	**7.** joyfully	**12.** growled
3. enjoyed	**8.** poorly	**13.** attitude
4. messy	**9.** enjoyment	**14.** scrawled
5. produce	**10.** valuable	**15.** joyous

/ow/ sound	Suffix -y	Words that share the same base word
4. _____	7. _____	10. _____
Suffix -ly	**Suffix -able**	11. _____
5. _____	8. _____	12. _____
6. _____	**Suffix -ment**	
	9. _____	

APPLY Fill in the blank with the spelling word that best completes the sentence.

enjoyed	flaw	messy	valuable	secure	poorly

13. The most _____ item in my bedroom is a book signed by Beatrix Potter.

14. There was a _____ in my essay, so I rewrote it.

15. Ava _____ last night's choir concert.

16. The rabbit's _____ cage needs to be cleaned today.

17. The jewels were _____ in the safe at the bank.

18. I did _____ on my quiz, so I will have to study harder next time.

Review

FOCUS
- A **pronoun** is a word that takes the place of a noun in a sentence. The pronoun must agree in number and gender with the noun it replaces.
- A **possessive noun** ends in an apostrophe s ('s). A plural possessive noun ends in just an apostrophe ('). A **possessive pronoun** does not use an apostrophe.
- A **contraction** combines two words. An apostrophe (') replaces letters that are removed when combining the two words.
- The **greeting** and **closing** in a letter begin with a capital letter. A comma is placed after the name of the person in the greeting and after the closing.

PRACTICE In the letter below, triple-underline the letters in the greeting and closing that need to be capitalized. Underline the pronouns and circle the contractions.

my dearest aunt sophia

Thank you for the birthday gift. I really like books. I'm always excited to have more of them to read. When I showed Juli the book you sent, she was happy too. She knew it was a book that I had wanted to buy. I'll let her borrow it when I'm finished with it. I can't wait to see you when you come to visit!

thank you

Daniel

APPLY **Rewrite the sentences below, replacing the underlined nouns with pronouns.**

1. <u>Hank's</u> shirt has a picture of a hawk on <u>the shirt</u>.

   _____

3. <u>Beatriz</u> gave <u>Beatriz</u> a haircut.

   _____

4. <u>Maxwell</u> walked <u>Maxwell's</u> dog around the block.

   _____

Rewrite the incorrect possessive noun correctly.

5. Gabriels shirt went into the dirty laundry. _____

6. The girls bicycles were out in the yard. _____

7. His wifes name is Addison. _____

8. His sons names are James, Oliver, and Owen. _____

Combine each pair of words to form a contraction, and use the contraction in a sentence.

9. we have _____

10. I will _____

11. could have _____

12. did not _____

13. are not _____

14. she is _____

The United States of America

Do you know why we celebrate the Fourth of July? It is the birthday of the United States! July 4, 1776, is the date the Founding Fathers adopted the Declaration of Independence.

Today the Unites States is a free country. But it was not so a long time ago. The United States used to be part of England. England made the laws and told people here how to live.

Many people did not like the way they were treated by England. The laws were not fair. They wanted to be free, so they decided to fight for their freedom.

People explained their reasons for starting a new country by writing the Declaration of Independence. Thomas Jefferson, Benjamin Franklin, and John Adams helped write it.

The Declaration of Independence is one of the most important writings in the history of the United States. It declared that people were free to make new rules. It talks about many of the freedoms we enjoy today. It says that all people are created equal. It also explains our rights such as "life, liberty, and the pursuit of happiness."

The leaders in the early United States of America had to make many decisions to set up their government. Some of them thought that each state should have its own government. Others believed that the states should come together to form one government. Smaller states were afraid that larger states would have too much power.

In May of 1787, the leaders of the United States met for a convention. We call this group of leaders the Founding Fathers. Many of them helped write the Declaration. They were farmers, lawyers, or traders. They all wanted to make a new set of laws that would keep the United States free.

Leaders from most states traveled to Philadelphia. Their job was to write the Constitution. The Constitution was a set of laws for the new country. It took a while to write.

In September of 1787, the Constitution was finally finished. Nine states had to approve it before it became law. This happened in June of 1788.

The Constitution explains the rights and duties of all citizens. It also tells how our government works. It set up the three branches of government, each with different powers. Each branch watches over the other two branches.

The Constitution is a living document. This means that people can make changes to it. The founders had to make some changes. Some people thought the Constitution did not protect people's rights. They wanted to add a new part to the Constitution to do this, and the founders agreed to update it.

Changes to the Constitution are called amendments. The founders added ten amendments. The first ten amendments are called the Bill of Rights.

The Declaration, the Constitution, and the Bill of Rights have granted Americans the freedoms that we have today. It is because of those freedoms that we celebrate the birth of this country on the Fourth of July.

Vocabulary

> **Focus** Review the vocabulary words from "Aesop and His Fables."

desperately	guaranteed	shame
determined	persistent	shuffled
fashioned	persuasion	sign
flash	plodded	transitioned
glorious	settle	

PRACTICE Synonyms mean the same or nearly the same thing. Write the vocabulary word that is a synonym for each group of words.

1. encouragement, convincing, _____

2. extremely, seriously, _____

3. mark, signal, _____

4. changed, altered, _____

5. scuffled, shambled, _____

6. agree, decide, _____

APPLY An *adage* is a traditional, wise saying. Use a vocabulary word to complete the explanation of each adage below.

7. *Practice makes perfect* means that a _____ and _____ person who keeps working on something will eventually get it right.

8. *Too many cooks spoil the broth* means that when anything is _____ by too many people, it does not come out right.

9. *Stop and smell the roses* means that you should take the time to enjoy the beautiful and _____ things in life, even if you are busy.

10. *Nothing ventured, nothing gained* means that if you do not try to do something, you are _____ to fail at it—so you should always try.

11. *Slow and steady wins the race* means that the person who _____ along slowly and surely will likely win.

12. *Fool me once,* _____ *on you; fool me twice, shame on* me means that a person should be embarrassed if that person keeps getting tricked in the same way.

Cause and Effect

> **FOCUS**
> - A **cause** is *why* something happens.
> - An **effect** is *what* happens.

PRACTICE Read each sentence. Read each cause.
Write a possible effect.

1. **Cause:** The sun felt very hot to the people at the beach.

   Effect: _____

2. **Cause:** The farmland had no rain for several months.

   Effect: _____

3. **Cause:** The boy lost all his money.

   Effect: _____

4. **Cause:** The girl missed the bus.

   Effect: _____

APPLY Read each effect from a fable in "Aesop and His Fables." Write a cause from to complete each sentence.

5. The cold wind made the man pull his cloak around himself. But because _____, the man took off his cloak.

6. Because _____, the crow was able to drink the water in the pitcher.

7. Because _____, the man and his son kept changing who did or did not ride the donkey.

At the end of "Aesop and His Fables," Aesop encourages the children to go home and be storytellers. Think about this as a cause. Write an effect that you think might happen after the story ends.

8. _____

_____

_____

Graphic Organizer Resources

Name _____ **Date** _____

Cause and Effect

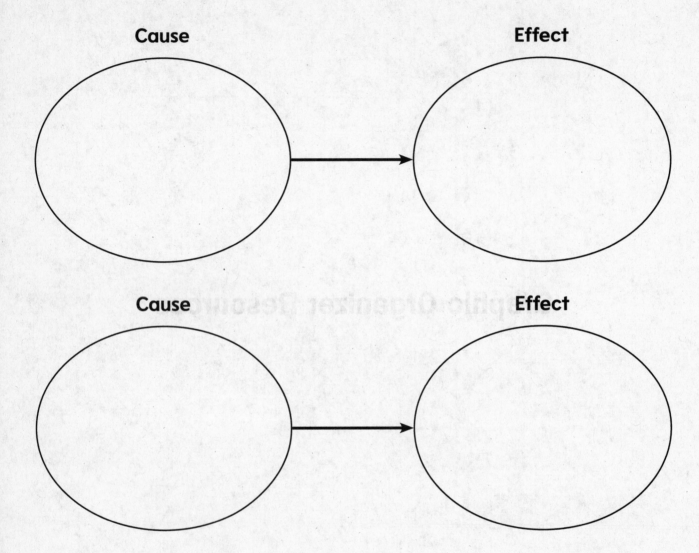

Cause

Effect

Cause

Effect

Compare and Contrast

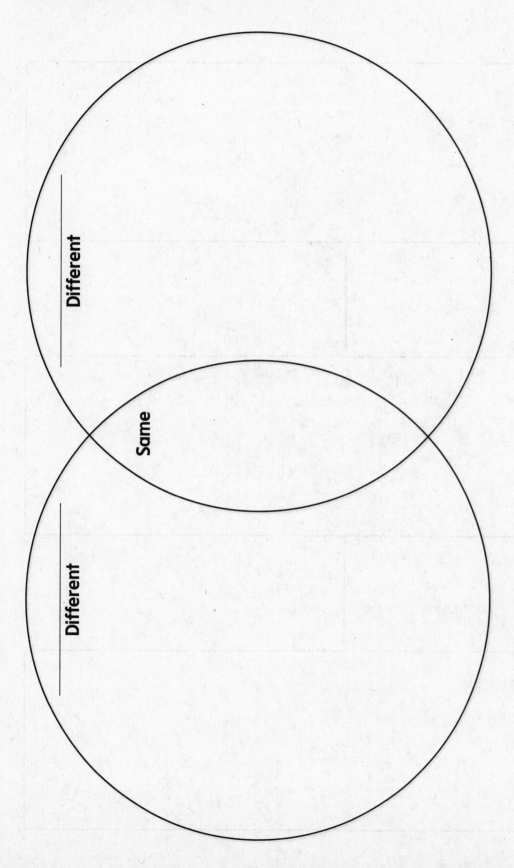

Sequence

First

```
┌──────────────────────────────────────────────┐
│                                                │
│                                                │
│                                                │
│                                                │
└──────────────────────────────────────────────┘
```

Next

```
┌──────────────────────────────────────────────┐
│                                                │
│                                                │
│                                                │
│                                                │
└──────────────────────────────────────────────┘
```

Last

```
┌──────────────────────────────────────────────┐
│                                                │
│                                                │
│                                                │
│                                                │
└──────────────────────────────────────────────┘
```

Fact and Opinion

Fact	Opinion

Making Inferences

Inference

[ ]

=

Prior Knowledge

[ ]

+

Clue

[ ]

Story Map

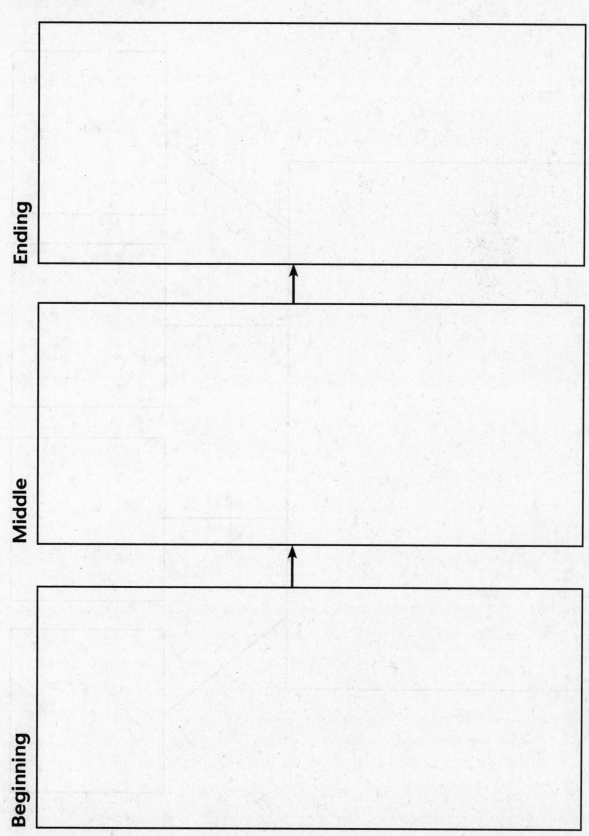

Ending

Middle

Beginning

Word Map 1

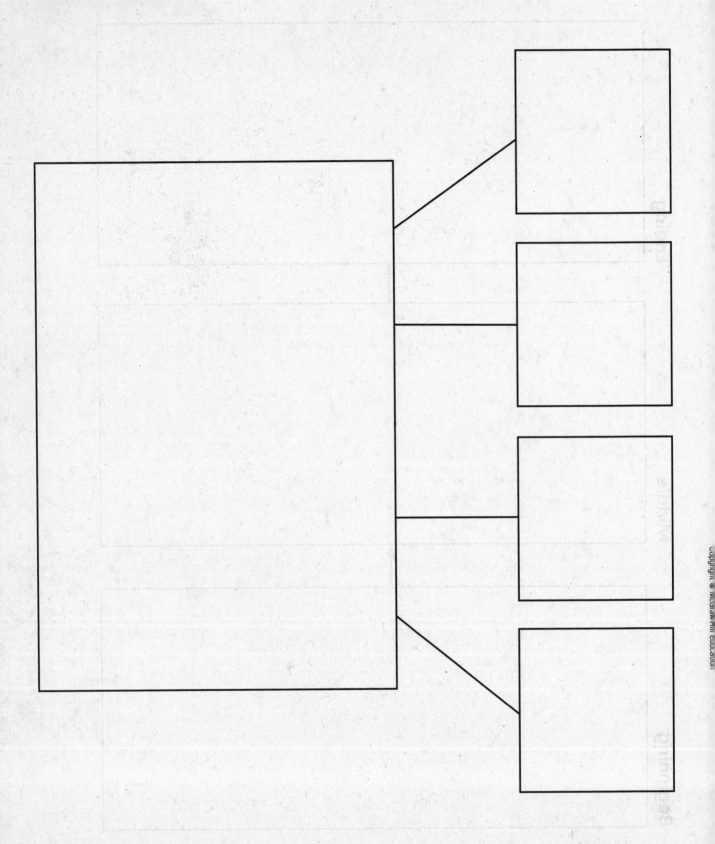

Word Map 2

TREE

T	*Topic Sentence—Tell what you believe.*
R **First Reason** **E**	*Reasons—Three or more. Explain each reason further.* **Reason:** **Explanation:**
Second Reason	**Reason:** **Explanation:**
Third Reason	**Reason:** **Explanation:**
E	*Ending—Wrap it up right.*

WWW-H2-W2

W	**W**ho are the characters in the story?
W	**W**hen does the story take place?
W	**W**here does the story take place?
H	**H**ow do the characters react at different points in the story?
H	**H**ow does the story end?
W	**W**hat does the main character want to do?
W	**W**hat happens in the story?

Idea Web

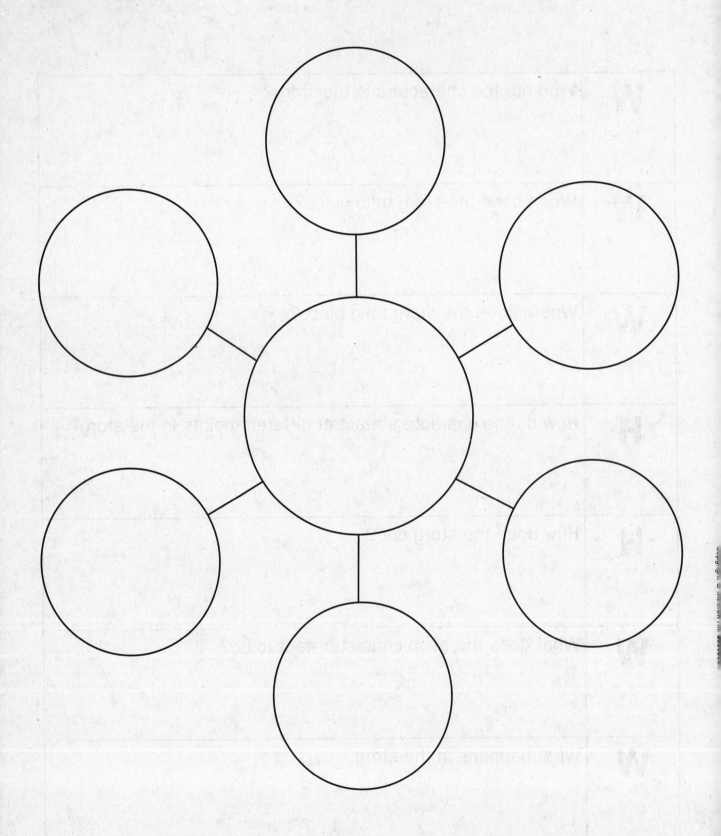